The Living God

A Catechism for
the Christian Faith
Volume 2

Translated from the French by
Olga Dunlop

ST VLADIMIR'S SEMINARY PRESS
CRESTWOOD, NEW YORK 10707
1996

Library of Congress Cataloging-in-Publication Data

Dieu est vivant. English
  The Living God: a catechism for the Christian faith/translated from the French by
Olga Dunlop.
    p. cm.
    Translation of: Dieu est vivant.
    ISBN 0-88141-040-3 (set)
    1. Orthodox Eastern Church—Catechisms—English. 2. Orthodox Eastern
Church—Doctrines. 3. Orthodox Eastern Church—Liturgy. I. Title.
BX345.D51413 1989
238© 19—dc20

Originally published in French under the title
Dieu est Vivant
by Editions du Cerf

Translation © 1989 by
ST VLADIMIR'S SEMINARY PRESS
CRESTWOOD, NY 10707
1-800-204-2665

Second printing 1996

ISBN 0-88141-009-8 Vol 1
ISBN 0-88141-010-1 Vol 2
ISBN 0-88141-040-3 (Set)

PRINTED IN THE UNITED STATES OF AMERICA

Contents

Part VI

Ascension and Pentecost

The New Era of the Church

CHAPTER 16

THE ASCENSION

We are told about the Ascension by St Luke, who speaks of it at the end of his Gospel (24:50-52) and also at the beginning of the Acts of the Apostles (1:1-11), which he wrote. St Mark also talks about it, but more briefly, in the last chapter of his Gospel (16:19).

We already know[1] that forty days after His Resurrection, Jesus appeared to the disciples for the last time. On this day, the day of the Ascension, He spoke to them at great length.

A) Jesus Speaks to Them About the Reign of the Messiah

When the disciples asked Him, "Lord, will you at this time restore the kingdom to Israel?" (Acts 1:6), Jesus answered, "It is not for you to know times or seasons which the Father has fixed by His own authority." Furthermore, Jesus had already told His disciples on the evening of Holy Thursday, "In My Father's house are many rooms; if it were not so, would I have told you that I go to prepare a place for you? And when I go and prepare a place for you, I will come again and will take you to Myself, that where I am you may be also" (Jn 14:2-3). Thus the reestablishment of the kingdom of Israel, for which the disciples were waiting, will actually come about when they enter the Father's house with Christ, the King of Israel. The reign of the Messiah, which David's kingdom had prefigured, and which Israel had been expecting since the great prophet Isaiah had so forcefully foretold it in 740 B.C., has actually been initiated by Christ's first coming. But it will be fully triumphant only at the Second Coming.[2]

1. See Part V, chapter 14, p. 219.
2. See Part VII.

B) He Entrusts Them With a Mission

The disciples must prepare and hasten this return (cf 2 Pet 3:12), this second coming of Christ the King, by accomplishing the mission which Jesus entrusted to them: "You shall by My witnesses in Jerusalem and in all Judea and Samaria and to the ends of the earth" (Acts 1:8). We are also reminded of this mission at the end of the Gospel of St Matthew (28:19-20): "Go therefore and make disciples of all nations, baptizing them in the name of the Father and of the Son and of the Holy Spirit, teaching them to observe all that I have commanded you; and lo, I am with you always, to the close of the age." We must keep in mind that in those days the means of communication were very primitive. The apostles, who were poor men, simple fishermen by trade, traveled on foot, and it seems incredible that Jesus should have asked them to go "to the ends of the earth." But, in fact, they succeeded in doing so. Their teaching reached not only to the ends of the earth, as it was known at their time, but through the disciples of their disciples it has been spread throughout the whole world. Even today, at our baptism we promise to obey this command of the risen Christ given just before His Ascension and thus become witnesses of His Resurrection.

C) He Tells Them That to be Able to Accomplish This Mission They Will be Given "Power From on High"

"He charged them not to depart from Jerusalem, but to wait for the promise of the Father, which, He said, 'you heard from Me, for John baptized with water, but before many days you shall be baptized with the Holy Spirit . . . You shall receive power when the Holy Spirit has come upon you'" (Acts 1:4-5,8), "power from on high" (Lk 24:49). It is God the Holy Spirit who will visit them. He had already promised this on Holy Thursday evening. "And I will pray the Father, and He will give you another Counselor . . . even the Spirit of truth . . ." (Jn 14:16-17). "It is to your advantage that I go away, for if I do not go away, the Counselor will not come to you; but if I go I will send Him to you" (Jn 16:7). "He will teach you

(handwritten margin notes: "Was there no Spirit within the people that did just not recognize the Spirit within them")

all things, and bring to your remembrance all that I have said to you" (Jn 14:26). "When the Spirit of truth comes, He will guide you into all the truth" (Jn 16:13). "But when the Counselor comes, whom I shall send to you from the Father, even the Spirit of truth, who proceeds from the Father,[3] He will bear witness to Me; and you also are witnesses . . ." (Jn 15:26-27).

After having spoken to them in this way, "He led them out as far as Bethany, and lifting up His hands He blessed them. While He blessed them He parted from them, and was carried up into heaven" (Lk 24:50-51). "So then the Lord Jesus . . . was taken up into heaven, and sat down at the right hand of God"[4] (Mk 16:19). This is what we call the Ascension.

"And while they were gazing into heaven as He went, behold, two men stood by them in white robes, and said, 'Men of Galilee, why do you stand looking into heaven? This Jesus, who was taken up from you into heaven, will come in the same way as you saw Him go into heaven'" (Acts 1:10-11). Then the disciples "returned to Jerusalem with great joy" (Lk 24:52).

Why were these men full of joy rather than sorrow at the departure of their beloved Master? They were joyful, first of all, because they had just received a wonderful promise from God's own messengers, "He will return." Furthermore, had He not promised just before leaving to send them "the other Comforter," one who would fill them with truth and joy?

But most of all, they knew that the one who was taken away from them was alive, that He would be with them to the end of time and that He had gone to prepare a place for them with the Father. He had been taken up in His human nature (which is their nature and our nature), in His glorified human body (which is their body and our body). Christ's body ascended into heaven and opened heaven's Royal Doors to all. We also will be able to pass through these doors

---

3. It is from this revelation of Christ that the following passage of the Creed is taken: "I believe . . . in the Holy Spirit, . . . who proceeds from the Father."

4. This phrase is repeated in the Creed: "[He] ascended into heaven, and sits at the right hand of the Father." This is called "the Sitting at the right hand" in the anaphora of the Divine Liturgy.

and to sit, like Christ, at the right hand of the Father. The doors
of heaven are now open to all mankind:

> Lift up your heads, O gates!
>   and be lifted up, O ancient doors!
>   that the King of glory may come in.
> Who is the King of glory!
>   The Lord, strong and mighty,
>   the Lord, mighty in battle!
> Lift up your heads, O gates!
>   and be lifted up, O ancient doors!
>   that the King of glory may come in.
> Who is this King of glory?
>   (Ps 23 [24]:7-10)

Through His Ascension, Christ has reconciled our human and
heavenly bodies, which had been torn apart as a result of man's
sinfulness. That is why in the seventh ode of the matins canon for
the feast we exclaim: "Taking the fallen nature of man upon Thy
shoulders and ascending with it, O Savior, Thou didst bring it to God
the Father!" And in the eighth ode we sing: "Our fallen nature has
been elevated above the angels and is established on the divine throne
in a manner which surpasses all understanding."

The Ascension completes the work of the Son begun at the Annunciation. Having taken upon Himself our fallen human nature, "the
form of a servant, . . . He humbled Himself and became obedient
unto death, even death on a cross. Therefore God has highly exalted
Him" (Phil 2:7-9), and our nature with Him. The Ascension is also
the glorification of Christ, who had been humiliated at the time of
the Passion, so that "at the name of Jesus every knee should bow,
in heaven and on earth and under the earth, and every tongue confess
that Jesus Christ is Lord, to the glory of God the Father" (Phil 2:10-
11).

Finally, it is the glorification of our own nature which He came
to raise again and to save from degradation and death.

Knowing all this, how could the disciples not be filled with "great
joy"?

CHAPTER 17

THE ICON AND TROPARION
OF THE ASCENSION

Let us now try to gain a deeper understanding of the meaning of the Ascension by looking at the icon of the feast and listening to the troparion which hymns it.

Sage: In the upper part of the icon, in the center of several large concentric circles (called "mandorla") which symbolize heaven, you see Christ sitting in majesty. He gives the blessing with His right hand, while in His left He holds a scroll, representing the word which He taught while on earth. An angel stands on either side of Him.

Seeker: Yes, and I also see that Christ is wearing a white or rather golden tunic just like the one on the icon of Pascha.

Sage: We see Christ similarly dressed on the icon of the Transfiguration too. The luminous color of the tunic symbolizes the glorious body of Christ and indicates that after the Resurrection, He has a body which is no longer subject to the laws and needs of earthly beings. He is also free of the law of gravity.

You have noticed the color of Christ's tunic, now look at the garments of the other figures.

Seeker: The garments of the angels who are carrying Christ are the same color as those of the apostles, while the two angels standing beside the Virgin are wearing white tunics.

Sage: The two angels in red garments bear witness to the Incarnation and the Passion, because even though Christ is ascending into heaven in His glorious body, this body still bears the marks of the Crucifixion. One of the Old Testament passages which is read during the vespers of Ascension (Is 63:1-3) perfectly describes this suffering and glorious Messiah, clothed in red as a symbol of His sacrifice:

Who is this that comes from Edom,
in crimsoned garments from Bozrah,
He that is glorious in His apparel,
marching in the greatness of His strength?
"It is I, announcing vindication,
mighty to save."
Why is Thy apparel red,
and Thy garments like his that treads in the wine press?
"I have trodden the wine press alone,
and from the peoples no one was with Me."

As for the two men clothed in white (Acts 1:9-11), they remind us of those angels who on the day of the Resurrection appeared to the women who came to Christ's tomb and announced that He was alive (Lk 24:4 and Jn 20:12).

Thus human nature, represented by the blood-and-earth-colored garments of the angels who are raising Jesus, is found in heaven. Whereas divine nature, represented by the white garments of the two angels who are speaking to the apostles, is found on earth. As St Athanasius tells us, "God became man, so that man might become God."

The two angels dressed in white foretell Christ's return in glory at the end of time. Sometimes they are represented holding a scroll upon which are written the words: "Men of Galilee, why do you stand looking into heaven? This Jesus, who was taken up from you into heaven, will come in the same way as you saw Him go into heaven" (Acts 1:11). According to the prophecy of Zechariah, which is read at Ascension vespers, the Second Coming will take place on the Mount of Olives (a hill across from Jerusalem), at exactly the same spot from which Christ ascended into heaven (Acts 1:12).[5] "On that day His feet shall stand on the Mount of Olives which lies before Jerusalem on the east" (Zech 14:4). On the icon this mountain is represented by some craggy boulders and four olive trees.

---

5. In his Gospel, Luke tells us that just before the Ascension Jesus brought His disciples "as far as Bethany" (Lk 24:50). The Mount of Olives, on which Luke locates the Ascension in Acts 1:12, is found precisely on the road to Bethany.

The Ascension of Our Lord

Kontakion of Ascension

Common Chant
arr. from LVOV-BAKHMETEV

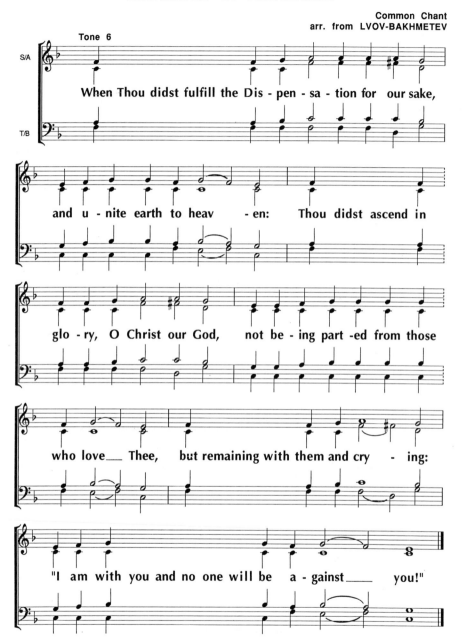

Seeker: It almost seems as if the mountains and trees cut the icon into two parts, with heaven and Christ in one part and the Theotokos and the apostles in the other.

But why are there twelve apostles? Judas betrayed Jesus and hanged himself (Mt 27:3-10; Acts 1:16-19) and Matthias was elected to replace him only after the Ascension (Acts 1:13-26).

Sage: You're right. There are twelve because the apostle Paul is represented with the eleven; he is standing on the left of the Theotokos. You can recognize him by his bald head and thin beard. On the right of the Theotokos you can see Peter, with short curly hair and a rounded beard. Paul is represented with the apostles because, although he did not live with Christ before His Passion, he did see the risen Christ on the way to Damascus. Paul represents the faithful who throughout the ages confess Christ in the Church. His presence on the icon shows that the church's vision is outside the limits of time; communion in faith in the Kingdom of God, through the grace of the Holy Spirit, has broken the temporal bonds of this world.

Seeker: Why are the apostles' garments both green and red?

Sage: Green is the color of hope and of the Holy Spirit. On Ascension Day Christ promised His disciples that the Holy Spirit would descend upon them. In Rublev's icon of the Trinity,[6] the angel who represents the Holy Spirit is also clothed in green.

As for red, it represents not only the earth and blood, as we already said, but also love.

Seeker: One group of apostles is pointing with their hands to Christ in heaven, while another group is looking at the Theotokos, who stands praying.

Sage: Depicted in this way, the Theotokos represents the Church.

Seeker: I see something else about the icon. It seems to me that it is divided into two parts vertically by the Mother of God and horizontally by Christ. Does this mean anything?

Sage: Let's take this observation and the one you made earlier about how heaven and earth seem to be separated by the mountain, and we can make an interesting observation: the figures of the Theotokos and her son form a cross which unites heaven and earth.

6. See Part II, p. 63

The olive trees are a symbol of nature glorifying God, because it is only as a result of Christ's sacrifice on the Cross that nature, which had been clouded through sin, can become luminous again.

As you see, "deciphering" an icon can be very interesting. However, we should not ascribe significance to every one of its characteristics or colors. An icon is the expression of a mystery of faith. By analyzing it in too great detail, we become overly intellectual and may forget that it should be an object of veneration. The existence of icons is possible because God became incarnate. Icons are here to teach us, to help us pray, and to express our faith in daily life. Finally, let's remember that everything we have discovered in this icon is summarized by the troparion of the feast:

> Thou hast ascended in glory, O Christ our God,
> granting joy to Thy disciples by the promise of the
> Holy Spirit.
> Through the blessing they were assured
> that Thou art the Son of God,
> the Redeemer of the world.
> (Troparion of the Ascension, tone 4)

Troparion of Ascension

Common Chant
arr. from LVOV/BAKHMETEV

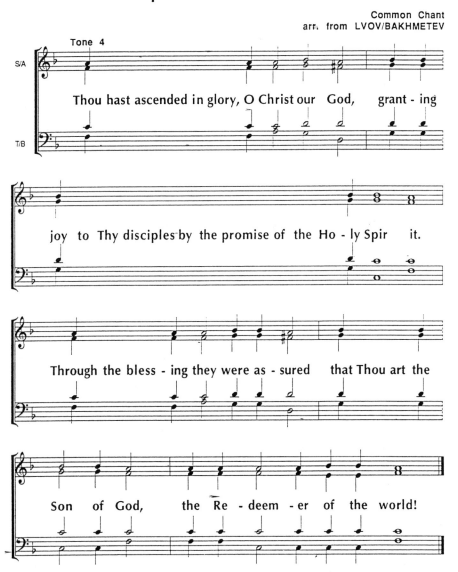

Thou hast ascended in glory, O Christ our God, grant - ing joy to Thy disciples by the promise of the Ho - ly Spir it. Through the bless - ing they were as - sured that Thou art the Son of God, the Re - deem - er of the world!

CHAPTER 18

The Holy Spirit in the Old Testament

We have just seen that on the day of His Ascension, the Lord Jesus promised to send His disciples another comforter, the Holy Spirit. This was not something entirely unfamiliar to the disciples because the Holy Spirit had already been mentioned quite often in the Old Testament.

Spirit is one way of translating the Hebrew word *ruah,* which can also be rendered as breath, wind, or even air and empty space. This vagueness in translation reflects the ambiguity in the meaning of this word in the texts of the Old Testament. The word spirit can also be applied to man. If the reference is to the spirit of God, it is sometimes called *Ruah Elohim.* The word *ruah,* which we meet at the very beginning of the Bible in Genesis 1 and 2, is translated in this way. Thus, in the following verse from the first chapter of Genesis, we read, "The earth was without form and void, and darkness was upon the face of the deep; and the Spirit of God was moving over the face of the waters."

The Spirit of God is the life-giving breath of God. "The Spirit of God was moving over the face of the waters." This evokes the image of a bird brooding over her chicks and protecting them by flying in circles above them. It represents the loving relationship between God and His creation. Even though the Spirit of God exists separately from His creation, He hovers above it.

The same word *ruah* is translated as "the *cool* of the day" in the passage which describes the day on which God went to look for man in the Garden of Eden after the Fall. This particularly emphasized the divine environment in which Adam and Eve lived. However, it also expresses a vaguely defined and mysterious aspect of the *ruah,* which like the wind is an undefined cosmic reality of which God is the master.

God can send this breath down upon man to act as a life-giving force. The one upon whom the Spirit "rests" receives the power to prophesy and accomplish great exploits. This happened to Joseph (Gen 41:38) when he interpreted Pharaoh's dreams. It also happened to Balaam when he cried, "How fair are your tents, O Jacob" and blessed Israel (Num 24:2-9). Another passage from the Book of Numbers which is read at Pentecost tells us that the Spirit is sometimes bestowed according to need and request (Num 11:24-30). We are told that Moses could not continue to bear the responsibility of leading the people alone; therefore, following God's command, he assembled seventy elders at the tent of meeting. God then descended in a cloud, took some of the spirit that rested upon Moses, and put it on the seventy elders. Two of them, Eldad and Medad, were not present in the tent. Nevertheless, they also received the spirit and began to prophesy like the others. On the other hand, the story of Babel,[7] the anti-Pentecost, demonstrates how any enterprise carried out without the participation of the Spirit is doomed to failure. It can only result in confusion and war.

The *ruah* as a life-giving force becomes at once the sign and the gift of extraordinary power when it is bestowed upon someone through unction. This is the "royal *ruah*" which designates the king and invests him with supernatural power. The first to receive this unction was Saul, but the Spirit of God forsook him and was replaced by an evil spirit because he disobeyed the divine command. Then the prophet Samuel came to Bethlehem and, inspired by an inner voice from God, chose David, the youngest son of Jesse, to be king. He poured oil from a ram's horn upon him (1 Sam 16:1-13). Oil is the chosen vehicle of the Spirit because, like the Spirit, it permeates a surface after being poured out on it. From the moment that the holy oil was poured upon him, David became the Anointed One of God, God's Christ. And the Spirit became manifest in him long before he was recognized as king through the extraordinary exploits he performed, of which the best known is his combat with Goliath.

The princes of David's lineage were not always worthy of the unction they had received. The power from God was later given by

7. See chapter 20 below.

Him to the prophets; the royal *ruah* became the prophetic *ruah*. Thus Micah says, "But as for me, I am filled with power, with the Spirit of the Lord" (Mic 3:8).

Isaiah strengthened and expanded the religious aspect of the doctrine of God's gift of the Spirit through unction by foretelling the coming of the Messiah, the Anointed One of God, His Christ, the One upon whom the Spirit has rested since the beginning of time:

> There shall come forth a shoot from the stump of Jesse, and a branch shall grow out of his roots. And the Spirit of the Lord shall rest upon him, the spirit of wisdom and understanding, the spirit of counsel and might, the spirit of knowledge and the feat of the Lord. (Is 11:1-2)

And in Is 61:1-2, we find the words which Jesus applied to Himself in the synagogue of Nazareth, "The Spirit of the Lord is upon me, because He has anointed Me" (Lk 4:18-19). The One upon whom the Spirit of the Lord rests possesses the gifts of the Spirit and his reign is marked by justice (Is 11). It is a reign of peace which prefigures the end of time when "the wolf shall dwell with the lamb . . . The sucking child shall play over the hole of the asp . . ." These images symbolize the harmony and peace which are the fruits of the gift of the Spirit.

According to Ezekiel (36:25-28) the Spirit is not given only to this or that person. It concerns the whole people, gathered together from among all nations. It is also linked to a rite of purification by water and brings about a personal renewal. It is given to everyone individually, but only within the bonds of the community:

> A new heart I will give you, and a new spirit I will put within you; and I will take out of your flesh the heart of stone and give you a heart of flesh. And I will put My spirit within you and cause you to walk in My statutes and be careful to observe My ordinances . . . You shall be My people, and I will be your God.

Psalm 50 [51], a penitential psalm inspired by David's sin, also describes this regeneration of the sinful being through the Spirit. It is here that the spirit is first referred to as the "Holy" Spirit:

Purge me with hyssop and I shall be clean; wash me and I shall be whiter than snow . . . Create in me a clean heart, O God, and put a new and right spirit within me. Cast me not away from Thy presence, and take not Thy holy Spirit from me. (Ps 50:9, 12-13 [51:7, 10-11])

The prophet Joel takes up Ezekiel's idea of a collective *ruah* and foretells that the Spirit will fill the whole universe. St Peter cites him in his sermon on the day of Pentecost (Acts 2:16-21): "I will pour out My Spirit upon all flesh, and your sons and your daughters shall prophesy . . ."

In conclusion, we see that even though He is not yet clearly defined as a person, in the Old Testament the Spirit emanates from God Himself in the form of His breath. He penetrates the deepest recesses of man's soul to transform and regenerate him to enable him to obey the divine will.

CHAPTER 19

THE HOLY SPIRIT IN THE GOSPELS

First, let us go over the two great events of the New Testament in which the Holy Spirit manifested Himself and which we have studied in parts I and II.

A) The Annunciation

The archangel Gabriel announced to the Virgin Mary, "The Holy Spirit will come upon you, and the power of the Most High will overshadow you; therefore the child to be born will be called holy, the Son of God" (Lk 1:35). As soon as the Spirit overshadows the Virgin, the One upon whom He rests becomes present in her. For the Spirit has rested upon the Son from all eternity (see Is 61:1). The Virgin conceives the Son of God through the operation of the Holy Spirit: "The finger of the Father, the Holy Spirit, inscribes the Word on the virgin book, the womb of Mary."[8] The Holy Spirit makes Mary the receptacle of God, before making her the *Theotokos*, the one who gives birth to God.

B) The Baptism

St John the Baptist bore witness, "I saw the Spirit descend as a dove from heaven, and it remained on Him" (Jn 1:32; see also Lk 3:22; Mk 1:10; Mt 3:16). Jesus is the Christ because the Spirit (unction) rests upon Him and makes Him the Anointed One (Christ). Having been anointed by the Spirit, the Son will in turn

---

8. This is taken from the akathist sung in honor of the Virgin during Lent. Akathist means something to which we listen while standing.

be able to bestow Him upon us. In fact, He has become man so that He may bring the Spirit to us. This is what Jesus tries to explain to the Samaritan woman.

C) *The Conversation with the Samaritan Woman: The Gift of God*

This episode of the conversation of Jesus with the Samaritan woman is found in the Gospel of John (4:5-42). It is a very beautiful and spiritually profound narrative.

Jesus left Judea in the south and went north to Galilee. To get there he had to pass through Samaria, which separates the two provinces. He came to the town of Sychar "near the field that Jacob gave to his son Joseph." Being tired, he sat down at the edge of one of Jacob's ancient wells while the disciples went into the town to buy food. It was the sixth hour, that is, about noon, and very hot. The well was deep and its water excellent, but He had nothing with which to draw it. And so Jesus waited.[9] A Samaritan woman came by to draw water and Jesus asked her for a drink. We must remember that there was great animosity between the Jews and the Samaritans. This explains the woman's surprise, "How is it that you, a Jew, ask a drink of me, a woman of Samaria?" Jesus answered, "If you knew the gift of God, and who it is that is saying to you, 'Give me a drink,' you would have asked Him, and He would have given you living water." The woman showed no surprise at these extraordinary words but a change takes place within her. She adopts a different tone, calling Jesus "Lord." She asks, "Where do you get that living water?" and Jesus answers "Every one who drinks of this water will thirst again, but whoever drinks of the water that I shall give him will never thirst; the water that I shall give him will become in him a spring of water welling up to eternal life." The Samaritan woman wanted to drink some of this water so that she would never again be thirsty, but instead of answering, Jesus gave her a curious command, "Go,

9. One example among many showing that Jesus, our true God, is also true man: He gets tired and thirsty.

call your husband, and come here." The woman was very embarrassed and said, "I have no husband." Jesus pointed out that she had actually had five husbands and that she was not married to the man she was then living with. She did not deny the truth but said, "Sir, I perceive that you are a prophet," and immediately brought up a question of primary importance to her, "Our fathers worshiped on this mountain; and you say that in Jerusalem is the place where men ought to worship." In a flash Jesus' answer lifts us from the mundane level of this controversy to the heights of divine truth: "The hour is coming when neither on this mountain nor in Jerusalem will you worship the Father . . . The hour is coming, and now is, when the true worshipers will worship the Father in spirit and truth . . . God is spirit, and those who worship Him must worship in spirit and truth."[10]

What is this living water which Jesus promises to the Samaritan woman? What is the gift of God of which He speaks to her? Jesus Himself will give us an answer in the Temple of Jerusalem on the Jewish feast of Tents or Tabernacles.[11]

---

10. In this astonishing meeting between Jesus and the Samaritan woman we find all the stages of Christian initiation. The first is purification in baptismal water which is transformed into a gift of the Spirit. The second is illumination through the recognition of the Messiah as the Son of God, for the woman recognizes Jesus as the Messiah when He speaks of worshiping the Father. Finally, there is the union with Christ. In fact, is not the meeting at a well a nuptial image in the Bible (think of Rebekah and Isaac's servant, Gen 24: 15-27; Rachel and Jacob, Gen 29:9-14; Moses and Zipporah, Ex 2:15-22)? Every soul which meets God enters with Christ into the bridal chamber in the Kingdom of heaven (consider the parable of the ten virgins). After receiving this revelation the Samaritan woman becomes a witness to the faith and confesses Christ before others.

The Orthodox Church venerates the Samaritan woman as a saint, under the name Photina, "the one who bears the light." Her feast is celebrated on the fifth Sunday after Pascha, during paschal season which is especially set aside for baptism. In the Roman Church the Gospel about the Samaritan woman is read on the third Sunday in Lent in preparation for the paschal baptism.

11. This was an agricultural feast, for which large crowds gathered and lived for the week in booths made of green branches. It included supplications for rain; there were also rites commemorating miracles of water. Prophecies foretelling the coming of the spring which would regenerate Zion were also read: "On that day living waters shall flow out from Jerusalem" (Zech 14:8), and "the water was flowing down from below the south end of the threshold of the temple . . ."(Ezek 47:1).

D) *The Feast of Tabernacles: The Living Water (Jn 7)*

Jesus describes the living water in a dialogue with the Jewish people. We commemorate this event during the paschal period, on the Wednesday of the mid-feast. This day falls exactly halfway between Pascha and Pentecost. At the Liturgy we read the passage from John's Gospel which begins with the words, "About the middle of the feast Jesus went up into the temple and taught" (Jn 7:14). The icon for this feast depicts Jesus seated in the midst of the astonished elders, discussing the Scriptures. The Jews celebrated the Feast of Tents in the fall, so it does not coincide with the Christian feast of mid-Pentecost;[12] however, there are subtle similarities in the theme of both celebrations. The whole service of the mid-feast is a meditation on the words of Christ which are found a little farther on in the same chapter of John's Gospel, "On the last day of the feast, the great day, Jesus stood up and proclaimed, 'If any one thirst, let him come to Me and drink. He who believes in Me, as the Scripture has said, 'Out of his heart shall flow rivers of living water' " (Jn 7:37-38). The Gospel reading on Pentecost begins with the very same words. there can be no doubt as to the meaning of this "living water" because John explains immediately after, "Now this He said about the Spirit, which those who believed in Him were to receive." This living water, this gift of God, is the Holy Spirit. The Spirit rests upon the Son who in turn bestows Him upon mankind.[13] The Son

---

12. This presents us with a good opportunity to deal with a complaint we often hear nowadays, "What we really need is a good feast." The Church offers us this feast and invites us to celebrate it with joy. We often read in the Scriptures, "there was a feast," or "the feast day was approaching." Every feast marks a moment in the liturgical cycle. Listen to the choir and the reading, and you will recognize the feast which is being celebrated and understand its meaning.

13. In the mid-eleventh century there was a dispute between Rome and Constantinople over the procession of the Holy Spirit; in 1054 Cardinal Humbert, in the name of the Pope of Rome, excommunicated Michael Cerularius, Patriarch of Constantinople, in part over this issue.

    In the West a single word, *Filioque,* had been added to the Creed which both the Latin Church and the Orthodox had professed since the Ecumenical Councils of Nicaea (325) and Constantinople (381). *Filioque,* "and from the Son," meant that the Holy Spirit proceeds from the Father and the Son *(qui ex Patre Filioque procedit)*; the

of God became man so that He could send the Spirit to His brothers: JESUS GIVES GOD TO MAN. That is why, in the troparion for the mid-feast, we pray, "In the middle of the Feast, O Savior, fill my thirsting soul with the waters of godliness."

This troparion describes man's basic longing or thirst. The purpose of the entire "economy of the Son," that is, of all the saving actions of our regeneration by Christ, the Incarnation, Baptism, Transfiguration, Passion, Cross, Resurrection, and Ascension, is to assuage this thirst by preparing the way for the coming of the Holy Spirit at Pentecost. The Holy Spirit grants each one of us within the Church all those benefits which Christ obtained from the Father at every stage of His earthly life. Jesus Himself says, "He will take what is Mine and declare it to you" (Jn 16:14). We now understand how Christ's work is linked directly to the coming of the Holy Spirit. The Holy Spirit allows us to share in what Christ has acquired.

Orthodox continue to maintain that the Holy Spirit proceeds from the Father alone (see Jn 15:26).

Peter, Patriarch of Antioch, wrote to both Michael and the then pope, Leo IX, pleading for peace and communion between East and West. In his letter to the Patriarch of Constantinople, he observed that the Latins had confused the gift, descent, and mission of the Holy Spirit, which is the work of both the Father and the Son, with the procession of the Holy Spirit. In the first instance we are concerned with the descent of the Holy Spirit into the world; in the second, we are dealing with the origin of the person of the Holy Trinity from all eternity. Like the Son, He receives His being from the Father, who is the unique source of the Trinity.

CHAPTER 20

THE ANTI-PENTECOST: THE TOWER OF BABEL

To understand the real importance of what the Spirit brought mankind on the day of Pentecost, we must first become fully aware of the disordered condition of the world. It seems senseless and disorganized, like the scattered pieces of a gigantic puzzle whose form can no longer be discerned because its unity has been destroyed. Biblical revelation explains this breakup of a universe which the Creator had made a "cosmos." (In Greek, *cosmos* meant order and harmony before it acquired the secondary meaning of universe.) This story does not take place in historical time, but expresses a more profound truth by explaining the causes of this disorder. We are referring to the story of the Tower of Babel (Gen 11).

"Now the whole earth had one language and few words." During their wanderings about the earth in search of sustenance, men came to the plain of Shinar in Mesopotamia (present-day Iraq). The abundant natural resources of this land, with its extensive palm groves at the edge of the Tigris and the Euphrates, assured a comfortable existence. And so they decided to settle down there. The availability of earth, water, and sun resulted in the discovery of brick making. "Come, let us make bricks, and burn them thoroughly" (Gen 11:3) or dry them in the sun, they said. There was also an abundance of bitumen, an asphalt useful as cement or mortar. In other words, they had all the necessary materials to construct big buildings and to erect a beautiful city. This city was Babel or Babylon, which at the end of the third millenium B.C. became one of the major centers of civilization. Its inhabitants enjoyed a high level of culture and were proud of their technical knowledge. The hanging gardens of Babylon were one of the seven wonders of the ancient world. Proud of their scientific knowledge and sure of themselves, the Babylonians were certain that they could reach heaven through their own efforts. And so they decided to build "a tower with its top in the heavens." They said, "Let us make a name for ourselves ["name" here means renown, authority, power] lest we be scattered abroad upon the face of the whole earth." They no longer needed God, they had science. And so instead of seeking God, they sought their own renown.

God smiled and said,

> Behold, they are one people, and they have all one language; and this is only the beginning of what they will do; and nothing that they propose to do will now be impossible for them. Come, let us go down, and there confuse their language, that they may not understand one another's speech." (Gen 11:6-7)

The men "left off building the city" and "the Lord scattered them abroad over the face of all the earth." And from that day the city was called Babel, from the word *balal,* meaning to confound or confuse—an ironic name for Babylon, which actually means "the door of the gods"—"because there the Lord confused the language of all the earth; and from there the Lord scattered them abroad over the face of all the earth" (Gen 11:9).

And so we are now scattered all over the world, separated from each other. We no longer understand each other. Races and nations, social classes and ideologies, hate, fight, and kill one another. There is no communication even within the family itself; men and women, parents and children, often feel that there is a barrier separating them from each other. Each one is imprisoned by his own egotism and feels that no one understands him. (But do you try to understand others?) We are plagued by alcohol, drugs, sexual debauchery, mass psychoses. By these artificial means man tries to free himself from an unbearable isolation, to break down the walls of his prison. But all is in vain; these efforts lead only to an even greater despair. Society is like a wheel without a hub; the spokes are broken and the wheel no longer turns. Nothing works. Having broken with the Creator, the hub around which society should turn, men can no longer communicate with each other. We no longer form an integral part of creation. The pride of Babel has destroyed unity among us and the harmony of the universe. As man fell, he dragged a polluted universe down with him.

Man has separated himself from God, but God does not abandon him. He allows man to discover the consequences of his pride and egotism and to experience the depths of anguish and despair; but He has also undertaken the re-creation of the fallen world. He has undertaken a "new creation" which is accomplished in two stages:

1. He sent down His Son, who became man in the Incarnation. The vices of the "old man" were nailed upon the Cross. Fallen human nature was resurrected and raised up to heaven at the Ascension. He has created a New Man, a new Adam, Jesus Christ, God and man.

2. He sent His Holy Spirit at Pentecost so that each one of us individually and all of us together might be grafted onto this New Man and "attain to the unity of the faith and of the knowledge of the Son of God, to mature manhood, to the measure of the stature of the fulness of Christ" (Eph 4:13).

CHAPTER 21

PENTECOST

Pentecost occurred on the fiftieth day (*pentekoste* in Greek) after the Jewish Passover and the fiftieth day after the Resurrection of Christ. This was also the day on which the Jews celebrated a great feast commemorating the giving of the Tables of the Law to Moses on Mount Sinai. Jerusalem was full of foreigners, Jews living abroad (called the "Diaspora"), who had come from all corners of the world to celebrate the feast.

Several days earlier, a group of about one hundred and twenty disciples had gathered together with the apostles and the Theotokos. At Peter's suggestion they had chosen a twelfth apostle to replace Judas. Two disciples were selected: Justus and Matthias. Both men had accompanied the apostles from the time of Jesus' baptism to the Ascension, and were witnesses of the Resurrection. After asking the Lord to show which of the two He had chosen, they drew lots and the lot fell on Matthias.

The disciples were waiting in Jerusalem for the coming of the Comforter whom Jesus had promised. They were full of joyful expectation. They would finally know Him of whom Jesus had said, "It is to your advantage that I go away, for if I do not go away, the Counselor will not come to you; but if I go, I will send Him to you" (Jn 16:7). Since Jesus had departed and now sat at the right hand of the Father (Mk 16:19), He could now fulfill His promise.

And so Jesus bestowed the Spirit upon them on the anniversary of the day that Moses had been given the Law, "for the law was given through Moses; grace and truth came through Jesus Christ" (Jn 1:17).

> When the day of Pentecost had come, they were all together in one place. And suddenly a sound came from heaven like the rush of a mighty wind, and it filled all the house where they were sitting.

The Descent of the Holy Spirit

Troparion of Pentecost

Common Chant
arr. from LVOV-BAKHMETEV

Bless -ed art Thou, O Christ our God,

Who hast re -vealed the fish -er -men as most wise

by send -ing down up -on them the Ho -ly Spir -it.

Through them Thou didst draw the world in -to Thy net,

O Lov -er of man,—— glo -ry to Thee!

And there appeared to them tongues as of fire, distributed and resting on each one of them. And they were all filled with the Holy Spirit and began to speak in other tongues, as the Spirit gave them utterance.

Now there were dwelling in Jerusalem Jews, devout men from every nation under heaven. And at this sound the multitude came together, and they were bewildered, because each one heard them speaking in his own language. And they were amazed and wondered, saying, "Are not all these who are speaking Galileans? And how is it that we hear, each of us in his own language? . . . [W]e hear them telling in our own tongues the mighty works of God." And all were amazed and perplexed, saying to one another, "What does this mean?" But others mocking said, "They are filled with new wine."

But Peter, standing with the eleven, lifted up his voice and addressed them, "Men of Judea and all who dwell in Jerusalem let this be known to you, and give ear to my words. For these men are not drunk, as you suppose, since it is only the third hour of the day; but this is what was spoken by the prophet Joel: 'And in the last days it shall be, God declares, that I will pour out My spirit upon all flesh, and your sons and your daughters shall prophesy, and your young men shall see visions, and your old men shall dream dreams; . . . And I will show wonders in the heaven above and signs on the earth beneath, blood, and fire, and vapor of smoke; the sun shall be turned into darkness and the moon into blood, before the day of the Lord comes, the great and manifest day. And it shall be that whoever calls on the name of the Lord shall be saved." (Acts 2:1-8, 11-17, 19-21)

And Peter praised the name of Jesus the Nazarene, "whom you crucified and killed by the hands of lawless men [the Romans]. but God raised Him up, having loosed the pangs of death [literally, of Hades] . . . [David] foresaw and spoke of the resurrection of Christ [Ps 15 (16)], that He was not abandoned to Hades, nor did His flesh see corruption. This Jesus God raised up and of that we all are witnesses. Being therefore exalted at the right hand of God, and having received from the Father the promise of the Holy Spirit, He has poured out this which you see and hear . . . Let all the house of Israel therefore know assuredly that God has made Him both Lord and Christ, this Jesus whom you crucified . . . Repent, and

be baptized every one of you in the name of Jesus Christ for the
forgiveness of your sins; and you shall receive the gift of the Holy
Spirit. For the promise is to you and to your children and to all
that are far off" . . . So those who received his word were baptized,
and there were added that day about three thousand souls.
(Acts 2:22-24, 31-33, 36, 38-39, 41)

This is the story of Pentecost as told by Luke in the second chapter
of the Acts of the Apostles. We also celebrate this event with thanksgiving, singing the troparion for the feast:

Blessed art Thou, O Christ our God,
who hast revealed the fisherman as most wise
by sending down upon them the Holy Spirit.
Through them Thou didst draw the world into Thy net.
O Lover of man, glory to Thee!
(Troparion for Pentecost, tone 8)

Of course this narrative raises certain questions. Let us try to
extend our understanding of the biblical text and meditate on its
meaning.

Seeker: I really do have a lot of questions. First of all, why did
the Holy Spirit take the form of tongues of fire?

Sage: The tongue is the instrument of speech; the tongue of fire
represents God's tongue. The disciple upon whom it rests will proclaim the Word of God. After the descent of the Holy Spirit, each
apostle becomes a bearer of the Word. That is why Peter immediately
began to proclaim the Resurrection of Christ, and the others told
of "the mighty works of God."

Seeker: Why is it written that the tongues were "distributed and
resting on each one of them"?

Sage: The gift of the Holy Spirit is personal; it was received
individually by each one of the disciples. And yet there is only one
Holy Spirit. This divine fire descends upon all (remember the fire
that descended upon Elijah's offering), but it is divided to show that
each one individually receives the Spirit.

Seeker: At Babel tongues were also divided!

Sage: Exactly! What happened at Pentecost is the exact opposite of what happened at Babel. At Babel human tongues were divided through pride, so that men no longer understood each other and were separated and dispersed.

At Pentecost, it is the gift of God which divides itself so that it may descend upon each one individually and reunite them all. All those who have received the Holy Spirit proclaim the same Word, the Word of God. They are understood by all because they speak all languages. All language barriers are broken by the Word of God; it is understood by all those who have received the gift of languages. This is explained to us by the kontakion[14] of the feast:

> When the Most High came down and confused the tongues,
> He divided the nations;
> but when He distributed the tongues of fire,
> He called all to unity.
> Therefore, with one voice, we glorify the all-holy Spirit!
> (Kontakion for Pentecost, tone 8)

Seeker: Why did the tongues of fire descend only on the disciples and not on everyone?

Sage: They descended on those whom Jesus had prepared to receive the Holy Spirit, on those whose hearts were united (Acts 1:14) through faith in the risen Lord Jesus: one must believe in the Giver to receive the Gift. The Spirit did not descend on the world because "the world cannot receive [Him], because it neither sees Him nor knows Him" (Jn 14:17). He descended on those whom the Lord Jesus had brought together because they had believed in Him. He descended upon the Church. The Spirit is a personal gift, which each one receives individually, but at a time when everyone is assembled together: "When the day of Pentecost had come, they were all together in one place" (Acts 2:1). Suddenly they underwent a radical change; they became conscious of the Word of God within themselves and began to proclaim His wonders in all languages. It is at this point

---

14. The kontakion is a short hymn (*kontos* means short in Greek), sung after the sixth ode of the canon at matins and during the little entrance at the Liturgy: it sums up the meaning of the celebration.

that Peter courageously preached the Resurrection of the Crucified
One to those who had crucified Him.

Pentecost is still with us today. The Holy Spirit has been continu-
ously present since that time, coming down to consecrate those who
bear witness to the Resurrection of Christ. And He will be with us
till the end of time, as St Simeon the New Theologian, who lived
in the tenth century, tells us:

> A priest-monk who took me into his confidence once told me that
> he never served liturgical services without seeing the Holy Spirit,
> just as he saw Him when the metropolitan pronounced over him
> the prayer of initiation [into the monastic brotherhood] at the
> moment the sacred book was placed upon his head. I asked him
> in what form he had seen him? He answered: "The image was
> primitive and without form; nevertheless it was like a light. And
> when I myself saw what I had never seen before, I was startled,
> and I began to reason within myself, saying: "what can that possibly
> be?" At that moment, mysteriously but in a clear voice, He said
> to me: "I descend in this way upon all the prophets and apostles,
> as I do upon all the present elect of God and upon the Saints: for
> I am the Holy Spirit." [15]

The assembly of those who bear witness to the Resurrection of Christ—
those elected by God, whom the Holy Spirit consecrates—is the Church.
And each one of us is called to become one of these elect. Pentecost is
continually present within the Church. [16]

---

15. St Symeon the New Theologian, Sermon 184.
16. Church, *ecclesia* in Greek, means the assembly of those who are called.

CHAPTER 22

THE CHURCH

A) What the Church Is Not

Seeker: I thought that the Church was simply the house of God.

Sage: No. The house of God (*naos* in Greek, which comes from *nays*, ship) is the building or temple which houses the Church. A building is made of wood or stone, and wood and stones are material things. But the Church is composed of men and women and angels, of "living stone" as St Peter tells us (1 Pet 2:5). It is certainly appropriate for Peter to make this statement since he himself was called "Peter" (which means rock) by Jesus Christ. After he told Jesus, "You are the Christ, the Son of the living God" (Mt 16:16), Jesus called on him to become "a living rock" placed on the "corner stone" which is Christ Himself (1 Pet 2:6-7). Jesus then said to him, "You are Peter, and on this rock [that is, on you who recognize Me as Christ and Son of God] I will build My Church" (Mt 16:18). And the Church is in fact built of living stones who, following Simon Peter's example, believe in the Lord as Christ and God.

Seeker: I understand. The Church is the assembly of apostles, bishops, and priests who carry on Christ's work.

Sage: No! A bishop can only be the bishop of a city or of a group of people. He cannot be a bishop alone, just as a head cannot exist without a body. In the same way a priest must serve a parish or a monastery. A father can be a father only if he has children.

B) What the Church Is

The Church is the assembly of all the disciples of the Lord Jesus, whether they are still on earth or are in the Father's house, reunited around the Master. The word "church" is derived from the Greek word *ekklesia,* which in ancient Athens denoted the citizens' assembly.

Seeker: But since the Master has ascended into heaven, how can His disciples on earth be reunited around Him?

Sage: Where the Holy Spirit is, there also is the Son. Have you already forgotten the Lord Jesus' promise at the time of His Ascension, "I am with you always, to the close of the age?" But how is He with us? He is present through the Holy Spirit, for as we have already said, the Holy Spirit will "Bring to your remembrance all that I have said to you" (Jn 14:26). He makes us part of everything which is in Jesus and "will bear witness to Me" (Jn 15:26). Christ is present through the Holy Spirit. When the Holy Spirit descended upon the assembly of the faithful at Pentecost, the Word made His abode in them. They became the Church.

Seeker: I wish you would explain this more clearly.

Sage: Pentecost may be compared to the Annunciation and the Church to the Virgin Mary.

Seeker: In what way?

Sage: On the day of the Annunciation the Word became flesh of the Holy Spirit (Jn 1:14; Mt 1:18). The Virgin Mary conceived Jesus.

At Pentecost the same Holy Spirit descended upon the believers in the form of tongues of fire. The same Word came to make His abode within the Church and the Church began to proclaim the Word of God, to announce the Resurrection. The Church bears the Word and announces the Word, just as the Virgin carried and gave birth to Him. The Word is a Person, the Logos; it is God speaking to us, it is the Son present in the Church, just as He was present in the Virgin's womb.

Thus, since the time of Pentecost, the Spirit creates the Church; that is, He transforms an assembly of believers into a place where Christ is present. "Truly, I say to you . . . where two or three are gathered in My name, there am I in the midst of them" (Mt 18:20).

Where the Church is, there also is the Spirit of God and where the Spirit of God is, there also is the Church and all its grace. (St Irenaeus)

The Church is one even though the number of churches is constantly growing as It becomes more fertile. There are many churches but only one Church. (St Cyprian of Carthage)

He cannot have God as a Father who does not have the Church as a Mother. (St Cyprian of Carthage)

The Church is greater than heaven and earth. It is a new world and Christ is its sun. (St Ambrose)

The Body of Christ to which Christians are united through baptism is the source of our resurrection and salvation. (St Athanasius)

The Church is the terrestrial paradise in which the God of heaven dwells. (Germanus, Patriarch of Constantinople)

The Church . . . this great window through which the Sun of Justice shines upon a world of darkness. (St Nicholas Cabasilas)

Only the Church is of heaven. (A.S. Khomiakov)

Christ's Church is not an institution, it is a new life with Christ and in Christ, directed by the Holy Spirit. (Sergius Bulgakov)

The Church is the center of the universe, the place where its destiny is made. (Vladimir Lossky)

In the darkness of this fallen world, the Church is an opening in the wall made by the triumphant Cross. The love of the Trinity never ceases to shine through the light of the Resurrection. (Olivier Clement)

The Church is the entrance into the life of Christ, the communion with eternal life. (Alexander Schmemann)

The Church is the anticipation and sign of the Kingdom of God because, as with a seed or leaven, the realization of the Kingdom begins with today's Church. (Ignatius Hazim)

C) *The Church as It Seems To Be and as It Should Be*

Seeker: All this sounds very beautiful; but when I go to church I see people who cross themselves over and over again and then say vicious things about their neighbors. When my parents talk about the church, it's actually to tell stories about disagreements between priests. So where is the Holy Spirit in all this? How can I believe that Christ is living in this assembly of hypocrites?

Sage: If you had been in Jerusalem on that Friday when Pilate presented Christ to the crowd, covered with blood and spit, you would have thought that He looked repulsive. "As many were astonished at Him—His appearance was so marred, beyond human semblance . . . He was despised and rejected by men . . . and as one from whom men hide their faces" (Is 52:14; 53:3). This is how Isaiah described the suffering Messiah. His face was marked by all the ugliness of this world. The spitting of men disfigured Him and yet He remained the same Christ, the only Holy One. It is the same with the Church. It is disfigured by our spitting, our pettiness, our crimes, by the sins of those who belong to it, including yours and mine. And yet Christ remains hidden in it and the Spirit hovers over it. The Church is "Emmanuel," that is, "God with us", a God who consents to be present among sinners, publicans, and prostitutes. It is not those who are well but those who are sick who need healing, the Lord Jesus would say when He was criticized for sitting down at the sinners' table.

Seeker: I believe in God, I believe in Jesus Christ, but I don't believe in the Church.

Sage: Then you're confining God to heaven. The Christian God is a God made man, God among us, God hidden among men so that He may heal them. He is a God who acts and makes Himself known through those whom He came to save, those who never cease making a caricature of Him. His Word is heard among men and it is through them that He manifests His love. His is a God born in the stable at Bethlehem, a God crucified between two criminals, "numbered with the transgressors" (Is 53:12). If you cannot recognize the Holy One hidden among the sinners of His Church and in the shame of His Passion, you will not be able to recognize Him at His glorious Second Coming.

When we say in the Creed, "I believe in one, holy, catholic, and apostolic Church," we do not mean that we believe in what we see.

What a non-believing sociologist or historian can describe after studying the Church is not the object of our faith. We don't need faith to ascertain what we see. "Have you believed because you have seen Me? Blessed are those who have not seen and yet believe" (Jn 20:29). A stereotyped image of the Church at a certain place or time does not reflect its true essence and does not help us to define it.

The true object of our faith, what we really believe in, is God's word or promise. The Church is defined by the *creative Word of its Lord,* Christ, and the sanctifying power of the Spirit who brings this Word into existence. That is why the Church is holy in spite of the sins of its members.

We must understand clearly that it is the Word of the Creator who gives life to the creature. When God speaks, things are created; for example "Let there be light, and there was light." This is the source of a revealing phrase from the service for the dead, "Thy creating command was my origin and my foundation." Philaret of Moscow expresses this idea beautifully: "All creatures are balanced upon the creative word of God, as if upon a bridge of diamond; above them is the abyss of the divine infinitude, below them that of their own nothingness."[17] The most profound level of our being is defined by God's plan for us, by our vocation. We become fully realized as people only if we fulfill this God-given plan. By giving Simon, son of Jonas, the name Peter, Jesus lets him know what God wants him to become. *He is defined by his vocation.* Your true self is what God wants you to become, just as the building is the realization of the plan of the architect, and not the partially completed structure without roof or walls. It is the same with the Church: its true nature is defined by what God calls it to be. The pettiness and sins of Christian people pass away in the course of history, but the Word of God remains and never ceases to be heard in the sermons and church services. The Word of God is the permanent element in the life of the Church, defining its form and directing its development, despite the

---

17. Quoted in Georges Florovsky, *The Ways of Russian Theology* (Paris, 1937) (in Russian) cited by Vladimir Lossky in *The Mystical Theology of the Eastern Church* (Crestwood, NY, St. Vladimir's Seminary Press, 1976) p. 92.

mediocrity of its members. God Himself expresses this idea through the mouth of the prophet Isaiah:

> For as the rain and the snow come down from heaven, and return not thither but water the earth, making it bring forth and sprout, giving seed to the sower and bread to the eater, so shall My word be that goes forth from My mouth; it shall not return to Me empty, but it shall accomplish that which I purpose, and prosper in the thing for which I sent it. (Is 55:10-11)

To know what the Church really is, we should not describe the way it appears in some particular parish, diocese, or country, or at some particular time in history; rather we must study the way in which its Creator describes it. Through the constant action of the Holy Spirit, the Word of God continues to be creative in spite of the obstacles raised by man's sinfulness which delay the realization of God's plan. The saints whose feast day we celebrate on the Sunday after Pentecost make up the golden chain which manifests the power of this living word.

The Word of God calls on the Church to become:
1.   The Bride of Christ;
2.   The Body of Christ.

D) The Church as the Bride of Christ

The quasi-conjugal union which links God to His people and God's will to make the Church the Bride of His Christ is expressed throughout the Bible.

God Appears as the Bridegroom of His People Throughout the Old Testament

This theme was especially developed by the prophet Hosea who describes the characteristics which unite God to Israel and which are a foreshadowing of those which will unite Christ to the Church. St Paul emphasizes the continuity which exists between "Israel according to the flesh" (1 Cor 10:1-8) and the "Israel of God" (Gal 6:16).

Listen to the way God expresses His tender feeling for His people by the mouth of the prophet:

> And I will betroth you to Me for ever; I will betroth you to Me in righteousness and in justice, in steadfast love, and in mercy. I will betroth you to Me in faithfulness; and you shall know the Lord. (Hos 2:19-20)

Israel is already seen as the Bride of the Lord. But Hosea has no illusions as to the character of the Bride; the break between reality and God's plan is already becoming apparent. Israel is the wife of her Lord, but an adulterous wife, "a woman who is beloved of a paramour and is an adulteress" (Hos 3:1).

> Plead with your mother, plead—for she is not my wife, and I am not her husband—that she put away her harlotry from her face, and her adultery from between her breasts. (Hos 2:2)

But even though Israel, the Bride, betrays her Lord, He does not cease to love her with a divine tenderness, to correct her, to draw her back to Himself, and to sanctify her with His love.

> Yet is was I who taught Ephraim to walk, I took them up in My arms; . . . I led them with cords of compassion, with bands of love, and I became to them as one who eases the yoke on their jaws, and I bent down to them and fed them. . . How can I give you up, O Ephraim! . . . My heart recoils within Me, My compassion grows warm and tender. I will not execute My fierce anger, I will not again destroy Ephraim; for I am God and not man, the Holy One in your midst, and I will not come to destroy. (Hos 11:3-4, 8-9)

This conjugal union between God and His people will become even more fully and clearly realized in the New Testament.

Christ as Bridegroom in the Gospels

The parables told by the Lord Jesus show us that God will become the Bridegroom of His people through the Son.

1) The parable of the wedding feast (Mt 22:1-14)

In this parable the Kingdom of heaven is compared to a wedding feast which a king arranged for his son. Since those who were invited to the feast did not want to come, the king said to his servants, " 'The wedding is ready, but those invited were not worthy. Go therefore to the thoroughfares, and invite to the marriage feast as many as you find.' And those servants went out into the streets and gathered all whom they found, both bad and good; so the wedding hall was filled with guests" (Mt 22:8-10). It is no longer only the privileged who are invited to the wedding; the feast is not limited to a chosen people: both the good and the bad are called. All are invited to union with God who desires "all men to be saved and to come to the knowledge of the truth" (1 Tim 2:4). We do not yet know who the bride is; she is represented by all the guests. These guests are asked to wear special wedding clothes. When one of the guests takes advantage of the king's kindness and comes without a wedding garment, the king says, "Friend, how did you get in here without a wedding garment?" And he was speechless. Then the king said to the attendants, "Bind him hand and foot, and cast him into the outer darkness" (Mt 22:12-13).

What is this wedding garment which all the guests must wear when they come before the divine Bridegroom? How can the wicked enter the wedding chamber simply by changing their clothes? The beautiful exapostilarion[18] of the Bridegroom service which we sing at the beginning of Holy Week gives us the answer: "Thy bridal chamber I see adorned, O my Savior, and I have no wedding garment that I may enter. O Giver of Light, enlighten the vesture of my soul, and save me."

We must obtain a "robe of light" which is the gift of God. This gift is the Holy Spirit who is given freely to those who put their faith and trust in Christ, the Giver. When the Ethiopian asks the deacon Philip, "What is to prevent my being baptized?" Philip answers, "If you believe with all your heart, you may." And the

---

18. The exapostilarion is a hymn sung during matins between the canon and the praises; it summarizes the Gospel reading.

Ethiopian answers, "I believe that Jesus Christ is the Son of God" (Acts 8:36-37).

If we believe with our whole heart, if we have complete confidence in the merciful generosity of Christ the Savior, He will grant us the gift of the Spirit, regardless of our past sins. Through this gift we become members of the Church and are able to enter into the intimacy of the wedding chamber. Salvation is the conjugal union of believers, even those who had been "wicked," with Christ God, their beloved King.

This union is celebrated at a feast, a banquet, a celestial supper. We partake at the table of the Kingdom, we participate in this "Mystical Supper," when we communicate of the Body and most precious Blood of our Lord during the Divine Liturgy. Let us never forget that the Liturgy celebrates the union of love between Christ and His people. But the marriage is not yet consummated, as the parable of the ten virgins tells us.

2) *The parable of the ten virgins (Mt 25:1-13)*

The Bridegroom of the Church is late in coming. Ten virgins had been chosen to meet and escort Him with lighted lamps to the wedding feast. Five of them were foolish and said to themselves, "It is late, the Bridegroom will not come." They fell asleep and let their lamps go out because they did not have enough oil. They are like the people today who say, "We've been waiting for the Lord's Second Coming for two thousand years. At the Ascension He promised His disciples that He would return. We don't believe it any more; it's not true."

But the other young women were wise; they knew that even though the Bridegroom tarried, He would fulfill His promise. And so before going to sleep they made sure that they had enough oil for their lamps.

At midnight there was a cry, "Behold, the Bridegroom! Come out to meet Him." The wise virgins got up and trimmed the lamps which they had kept burning to meet the Bridegroom. The foolish virgins said to the wise, "Give us some of your oil, for our lamps are going

Behold, the Bridegroom

Kievan Chant

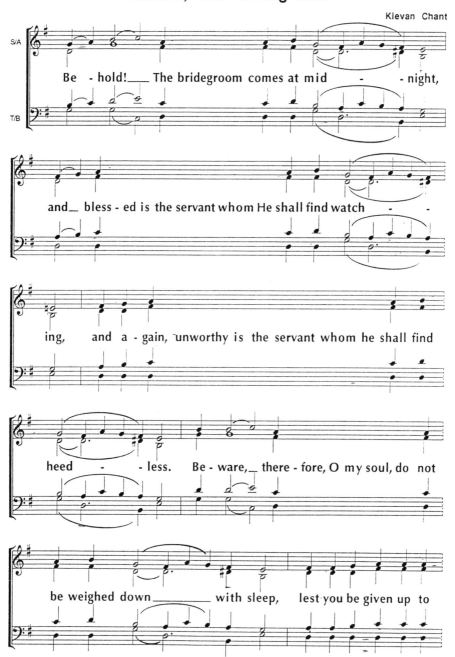

Be - hold!__ The bridegroom comes at mid - night,

and__ bless - ed is the servant whom He shall find watch - -

ing, and a - gain, unworthy is the servant whom he shall find

heed - - less. Be - ware,__ there - fore, O my soul, do not

be weighed down_____ with sleep, lest you be given up to

death and lest you be shut out of the king - - dom.

But rouse your-self crying: Holy, Holy, Holy art Thou, _____ O our

God! Through the Theo-to-kos have mer - cy on us!

out." But the wise replied, "Perhaps there will not be enough for us and for you; go rather to the dealers and buy for yourselves." And so when the Bridegroom came they were away, but those who were ready entered with Him into the marriage feast and the door was closed behind them. When the other virgins returned and cried, "Lord, Lord, open to us," He answered, "Truly, I say to you, I do not know you."

Christ will return only at the end of time. We do not know the day or the hour. Therefore we should be prepared to greet our Beloved at all times. The lamp of our hearts should always shine with the luminous presence of the Holy Spirit. Let us seek this holy presence and cherish it more than any material thing, for what good is it to gain the whole world, if we lose "Christ who is our life" (Col 3:4)?

We experience this parable with a particular intensity at the beginning of Holy Week, when we sing:

> Behold, the Bridegroom comes at midnight,
> and blessed is the servant whom He shall find watching;
> and again, unworthy is the servant whom He shall find heedless.
> Beware, therefore, O my soul, do no be weighed down with sleep,
> and lest you be given up to death
>   lest you be shut out of the Kingdom.
> But rouse yourself crying:
>   Holy, holy, holy, art Thou, O our God.
> Through the Theotokos, have mercy on us.[19]

Thus Christ has already become the Bridegroom of the Church, but He still bears the marks of the Crucifixion, and we must have faith to be able to recognize Him. He will appear as the Bridegroom to everyone only when He returns in glory. Then He will lead into the bridal chamber those who, hidden among the sinners of His Church, have recognized Him.[20]

19. Troparion of Bridegroom matins.
20. See Part V, p. 184.

The Church Is Revealed as the Bride of Christ in the Epistle to the Ephesians

There is continuous progress in revelation. Hosea described God as the Bridegroom of His people. In His parables Jesus reveals that it is through Himself that God becomes the long-awaited Bridegroom. In the Epistle to the Ephesians, the Church is identified for the first time as the Bride of Christ. The author of this epistle compares the love of a man for his wife with that of Christ for the Church. This is done to give a deeper significance to human marriage, but even more important, to illustrate the mystery of the Church. ". . . 'and the two shall become one flesh.' This mystery is a profound one, and I am saying that it refers to Christ and the Church" (Eph 5:31-32). *The Church is one flesh with Christ.*[21] Thus we are not linked to Christ as individuals but must together "attain to the unity of the faith," and in this unity realize "the fullness of Christ" (Eph 4:13). In other words, we are called to a double unity, unity with each other and unity with Christ. We are united to each other in Him, and by being united with each other we become one with Him. *One cannot be a Christian alone.* God cannot "know" us, in the sense that a man "knows" a woman, outside the community of the Church. We can enter into communion, into an intimate union with our Lord and God, only as a community,[22] as a Church, in which we love one another.[23] Together we constitute the Church, together we become one flesh with Christ.

The mystery of the Church is revealed, and the two great commandments of the Old Covenant, on which "depend all the law and the prophets" (Mt 22:40)—"You shall love the Lord your God with

---

21. We already have a glimpse of this in the magnificent marriage hymn of the Old Testament, the Song of Songs.
22. "For where two or three are gathered in My name, there am I in the midst of them" (Mt 18:20).
23. Before we recite the Creed together during the Liturgy, expressing the faith and love which unite us, the priest says, "Let us love one another, that with one mind we may confess . . ." and the congregation replies, "Father, Son, and Holy Spirit! The Trinity, one in essence, and undivided!" For we can confess the Holy Trinity only in love and brotherly unity.

all your heart, and with all your soul, and with all your might" and "You shall love your neighbor as yourself" (Deut 6:5; Lev 19:18; Mt 22:27, 29)—are expressed in their ultimate fullness in the marriage of Christ God to His Church.

This is the will of the Lord, "that He might present the Church to Himself in splendor, without spot or wrinkle or any such thing, that she might be holy and without blemish" (Eph 5:27). He knows that she has not yet attained this state. This is what He wants her to become; this is what she should become; this is what He makes her become; for He "gave Himself up for her, that He might sanctify her, having cleansed her by the washing of water with the word" (Eph 5:25-26). The Word which defines the being of the Church is accompanied by an outpouring of the Holy Spirit who fulfills this Word. But this fulfillment takes time and, as the Apocalypse tells us, the creation of the Church through the Word and the Spirit will be completed only at the end of time.

The Church Appears in the Fullness of Her Splendor in the Apocalypse: the Heavenly Jerusalem

Then I saw a new heaven and a new earth; for the first heaven and the first earth had passed away, and the sea was no more. And I saw the holy city, new Jerusalem, coming down out of heaven from God, prepared as a bride adorned for her husband; and I heard a loud voice from the throne saying, "Behold, the dwelling of God is with men. He will dwell with them, and they shall be His people, and God Himself will be with them. He will wipe away every tear from their eyes, and death shall be no more, neither shall there be mourning nor crying nor pain any more, for the former things have passed away." (Rev 21:1-4)

"Behold I make all things new . . . I am the Alpha and the Omega, the beginning and the end. To the thirsty I will give from the fountain of the water of life without payment." (Rev 21:5-6)

"Come, I will show you the Bride, the wife of the Lamb." And in the Spirit he carried me away to a great, high mountain and showed me the holy city Jerusalem coming down out of heaven from God, having the glory of God, its radiance like a most rare jewel . . . And I saw no temple in the city, for its temple is the Lord God the Almighty and the Lamb. And the city has no need of sun or moon to shine upon it, for the glory of God is its light, and its lamp is the Lamb. (Rev 21:9-11, 22-23)

The Spirit and the Bride say, "Come." And let him who hears say, "Come." And let him who is thirsty come, let him who desires take the water of life without price. (Rev 22:17)

"Surely I am coming soon." Amen. Come, Lord Jesus! (Rev 22:20)

Thus the Church is defined from the beginning by the creative Word of her Lord who is the Alpha, but also by the ultimate end to which this same Lord has predestined her, for He is the Omega as well.[24] This ultimate end (*ta eschata* in Greek) defines the Church to the same degree that her beginning does. Using theological terminology, we would say that we cannot ignore eschatalogical tension in defining the Church.[25] Her whole life is given direction only within the perspective of the heavenly Jerusalem, when the Bride will finally appear in all her splendor, reflecting the glory of her Bridegroom. The Church must pass from Alpha to Omega. She is able to do this, and she will do this, because she is loved with a creative and enduring love. We become truly ourselves, we blossom fully, only if we are loved. In spite of all the sins and failures of her members, the Church becomes truly herself, is transformed into the heavenly Jerusalem, through the love of her Creator. This Creator ceaselessly makes her grow by instructing her in His Word and by pouring the purifying and life-giving water of the Holy Spirit out upon her. Only then can she fulfill her true vocation: to take the world upon herself and save it, having been sanctified "for the life of the world."

---

24. Alpha is the first letter of the Greek alphabet; omega is its last.
25. "Eschatological" is everything which deals with the "last times," that is, the period of time that began with the coming of the Messiah and that will end with His return.

We think of all this on Easter night when we sing the hymn full of hope,

> Shine! Shine, O new Jerusalem!
> The glory of the Lord has shone on you.
> Exult now and be glad, O Zion.
> Be radiant, O pure Theotokos,
>   in the Resurrection of your Son.
> (Irmos of the ninth ode of the canon for the matins of Pascha)

E) The Church as the Body of Christ
The Cosmic Dimension of the Body of the Risen Christ

Before dealing with this chapter, we must set aside our habitual ways of thinking so that we can face a totally new reality: "Behold, I make all things new" (Rev 21:5). We are dealing here with what St Paul calls "a new creation" (Gal 6:15; 2 Cor 5:17). "If then you have been raised with Christ, seek the things that are above, where Christ is, seated at the right hand of God. Set your minds on things that are above, not on things that are on earth" (Col 3:1-2). The reader must put aside the concept of a world where objects are set next to each other in measurable space. "See to it that no one makes a prey of you by philosophy and empty deceit, according to human tradition, according to the elemental spirits of the universe, and not according to Christ" (Col 2:8).

We must "put on the new nature, which is being renewed in knowledge after the image of its Creator" (Col 3:10); "Christ is all, and in all" (Col 3:11). We must discover the cosmic dimension of this Christ in whom "the whole fullness of deity dwells bodily" (Col 2:9), He who is;

> the image of the invisible God, the first-born of all creation; for in Him all things were created, in heaven and on earth, visible and invisible, whether thrones or dominions or principalities or authorities—all things were created through Him and for Him. He is before all things, and in Him all things hold together. He is the head of the Body, the Church; He is the beginning, the first-

born from the dead, that in everything He might be pre-eminent. For in Him all the fullness of God was pleased to dwell, and through Him to reconcile to Himself all things, whether on earth or in heaven, making peace by the blood of His cross. (Col 1:15-20)

Paul certainly had to encounter the risen Christ on the road to Damascus[26] in order to attain the extraordinary intuitive understanding of Christ God according to the measure of this world of which He is Lord and Creator. In Him everything has its being, He is all in all, in Him dwells the fullness of all things, and in Him is embodied the fullness of the divinity. Such is the Body of the Risen One, "the spiritual body," as St Paul tells us in the first Epistle to the Corinthians. This Body is filled with the Holy Spirit. It is a heavenly Body even though it has been crucified and laid in the tomb. It is an incorruptible and immortal Body, a glorious Body which has been resurrected in glory (see 1 Cor 15:43, 53-54).

The Church is the Body of Christ

St Paul tells us that this Body is the Church (Eph 1:22-23; Col 1:18; 1 Cor 12:12-27). We must not think that St Paul uses this expression only as a literary image. He means that the Church is the mystical embodiment of believers in the cosmic Body of the risen Christ through the power of the Holy Spirit.

The Lord Jesus Himself told us that His Body would become the meeting place of the faithful, in a phrase which was distorted by the false witnesses at His trial before Caiaphas. They accused Jesus of saying, "I am able to destroy the temple of God, and to build it in three days" (Mt 26:61) or "I will destroy this temple that is made with hands, and in three days I will build another, not made with hands" (Mk 14:58). Actually, Jesus had said, "Destroy this temple, and in three days I will raise it up" (Jn 2:19). And the evangelist adds: "But He spoke of the temple of His body. When therefore He

---

26. Paul was thrown off his horse by a brilliant light. Falling blinded to the ground, he heard the Risen One say, "Saul, Saul, why do you persecute Me?" "Who are you, Lord?" he asked. "I am Jesus, whom you are persecuting" (Acts 9:1-18; 22:4-20; 26:12-18).

was raised from the dead, His disciples remembered that He had said this; and they believed the scripture and the word which Jesus had spoken" (Jn 2:21-22). In fact an attempt was made to destroy Jesus' body by nailing it to the Cross, and forty years later the Temple of Jerusalem was destroyed by Roman armies. Henceforth, the only temple, the only place where the true worshipers of the Father (Jn 4:23) assemble, is the Body of the Risen One.

Seeker: It all sounds pretty confusing to me.

Sage: Imagine, as St Paul does in 1 Cor 12:14-26, that each part of the body, the eyes, the head, or the feet could speak. Could the eye say to the hand, or the head to the feet, "I don't need you"? All the parts of the body are interdependent, each one needs the others. If one of the parts is ill, the whole body suffers together. And if a part works well (the lungs, for example, or the heart), the body as a whole profits from it. In the same way, we are all united to each other and to Christ within the Church. Various parts of a single body are attached to the head, which is Christ. If any member does or thinks evil, even unwittingly, the whole body, the entire Church, suffers from it. On the other hand, if anyone has a good thought or prays sincerely in the privacy of his room, the whole Church and all its members are healed by it.

We are all one within the Church and in communion with each other even though we may not be aware of it. The Holy Spirit moves throughout the Body of the Church in the same way that oxygen moves through the body of a person. Christ, the Head of the body, can move and direct its various parts as long as they are well. When we do evil, it is as if a part of the body becomes paralyzed: Christ no longer directs its movements, and the breath of the Holy Spirit no longer passes through it. On the other hand, when we listen to the Word of God, we receive impulses from the Head and are all able to communicate in love by the power of the Holy Spirit. Then we are united and are in communion with each other and with Christ.

The Church is the Eucharistic Bread, the Body of Christ

This perplexing mystery is realized and experienced in the mystery of the Eucharist. The New Testament reveals a double equation: the eucharistic Bread = the Body of Christ = the Church. The Body of Christ is the Church, but it is also the living Bread descended from heaven (Jn 6:51) which "gives life to the world" (Jn 6:33). This is "the bread of life . . . bread which comes down from heaven, that a man may eat of it and not die" (Jn 6:35, 50). This is the Bread which Jesus gave to His disciples on the eve of His death saying, "Take, eat, this is My Body which is broken for you for the remission of sins" (Mt 26:26; 1 Cor 11:24).

One can understand how the Church is the Body of Christ only by eating this Bread which is itself the Body of Christ. By communicating of the bread and wine, by communicating of the Body and Blood of Christ, Jesus' followers become themselves the Body of Christ, the Church. St Irenaeus uses the following image to illustrate this mysterious truth: just as water absorbs many grains of flour to make a single loaf of bread, so the Holy Spirit gathers the faithful to create a single body, the Body of Christ. The Mystical Supper, the Divine Liturgy, is the laboratory of the Church. It is here that God the Father molds the assembly of His children, the eucharistic assembly, using His two hands, the Word and the Spirit, to create a single loaf of bread, the Body of Christ, the Church. We are told the same thing in a slightly different way in the Epistle to the Ephesians (2:19-22):

> So then you are no longer strangers and sojourners, but you are fellow citizens with the saints and members of the household of God, built upon the foundation of the apostles and prophets, Christ Jesus Himself being the cornerstone, in whom the whole structure is joined together and grows into a holy temple in the Lord; in whom you also are built into it for a dwelling place of God in the Spirit.

Thus, the Church is seen as the assembly of believers who are nourished by the word of God and the Bread of Holy Communion. The Holy Spirit visits and gives life to this assembly, making it a single body with Christ as its Head and the believers as its members.

CHAPTER 23

THE MYSTERY OF THE DIVINE EUCHARIST: ITS ORIGIN, INSTITUTION, AND MEANING

We have just seen that the Bread of Communion, which is the Body of Christ, nourishes the Church and transforms it into the Body of Christ. The following two chapters will deal with this eucharistic mystery to which we have already alluded many times.[27] It would be helpful for the reader to begin by rereading these passages so that he might better understand these chapters on the Eucharist, the central aspect of Christian life.

The Israelites celebrated the *berakoth,* or blessings, through which they expressed their gratitude to God for His gifts. The servants of the Almighty must be able to recognize that a gift comes from God, and to commemorate this gift with gratitude (*eucharistia* in Greek, from which our word Eucharist is derived). It is through a perpetual act of thanksgiving that we acknowledge the work of the Creator, express our gratitude, and return glory to Him (*anapempo* in Greek, to send up but also to send back, send again) in the name of all creation. Through this eucharistic attitude, through gestures of gratitude, we humans, the conscience of all creation, recognize the link which unites creation to the Creator. Through this memorial of gratitude we maintain the flow of love between the Creator and His creation and, in doing so, restore the harmony of the universe.

Christ developed such a *berakah* or blessing on Holy Thursday at the supper with His disciples. This becomes very clear if we read St Luke's account of it (Lk 22:17-20) and compare it with the Jewish ritual of blessing a meal as it is described in the *Mishna.*[28]

---

27. See Part I, p. 29. Part III, p. 92. Part IV, p. 142. Part V, pp. 172, 174, 178, 213, 217.
28. The *Mishna* is a collection of Jewish prayers, instructions, and traditions. For a discussion

At the beginning of the meal the cup of wine is blessed with the words, "Blessed art Thou, O Lord our God, the King of all ages, who givest these fruits of the vine." That is why at the beginning of the meal, Jesus lifts up the cup for the first time saying, ". . . for I tell you that from now on I shall not drink of the fruit of the vine until the Kingdom of God comes" (v. 18).

Then, if there is no servant, the youngest member of the family brings a pitcher of water for the head of the family to wash his hands. This should have been done by St John, the youngest of the apostles, but Jesus took the pitcher from him and began Himself to wash the feet of the apostles (Jn 13:3-17).[29]

The head of the family would then take the bread and break it saying, "Blessed art Thou, O Lord our God, King of the Ages, who bringest forth the bread of the earth . . . Let us give thanks to our God, who has nourished us with His abundance." At this point Jesus "took bread, and when He had given thanks He broke it and gave it to them, saying, 'This is My body which is given for you. Do this in remembrance of Me'" (v. 19). Thus Jesus follows the gestures traditionally performed by the head of a Jewish family. However, He gives them a completely new meaning, identifying the bread with His body, which will be sacrificed for the life of the world upon the Cross.

After the meal the head of the family lifted the cup and blessed it a second time. That is why Jesus took the cup after supper saying, "This cup which is poured out for you is the new covenant in My blood" (v. 20). This explains the twofold blessing of the cup which only St Luke recalls. However, once again, Jesus gives it a new meaning by identifying the wine with the blood which He will shed upon the Cross and which will seal the New Convenant between God and man.[30]

---

of the meal *berakoth* see Louis Bouyer, *Eucharist: Theology and Spirituality of the Eucharistic Prayer,* trans. Charles Underhill Quinn, (University of Notre Dame Press, 1968), pp. 78-88.

29. See Part V, p. 172.

30. See Part V, 184.

St Paul completes St Luke's narrative (1 Cor 11:23-25) by adding, "For as often as you eat this bread and drink the cup, you proclaim the Lord's death until He comes" (11:26).

Thus we see that the blessing of the meal, and the offering of the bread and wine in thanksgiving to the God who had made them, parallel the offering which Christ makes of His Body and Blood upon the Cross on Great and Holy Friday. It is also associated with the conclusion of the New Covenant between God and His people, through Christ's sacrifice offered for the forgiveness of sins. "Do this in remembrance of Me . . . until I come"; the celebration of this meal will always be a memorial of thanksgiving for the Death and Resurrection of the Savior who leads His people into the Promised Land of His Kingdom. From the moment of Christ's Resurrection, it is through this Supper that we commemorate the whole act of salvation from the Passion to the Second Coming. But this commemoration (*anamnesis* in Greek, *zikkaron* in Hebrew) is not simply a memorial service, it is not an intellectual exercise. It is, above all, the participation of the congregation celebrating this "memorial" in the acts of salvation which are being commemorated. The Death, the Tomb, the Resurrection, the Ascension, the Sitting at the right hand of the Father, and the Second Coming of the Lord have eternal meaning. They take place in time, but they save man from the temporal. When we evoke these events in the Eucharist we forsake time to commune in "the worshipping act of the Body of Christ towards God, by which His eternal Kingdom 'comes' in time."[31]

This memorial, celebrated at a given moment in time, becomes a communion, a participation, in the eternal action of the Son through the action of the Holy Spirit. The Holy Spirit will "bring to your remembrance all that I have said to you" (Jn 14:26) and "will take what is Mine and declare it to you" (Jn 16:14). Thus it is through the Holy Spirit that representation becomes participation and communion.

Now we can understand the importance of the Liturgy. Through it we participate in everything that Christ has done, is doing, and

---

31. Dom Gregory, Dix, *The Shape of the Liturgy,* 2nd ed., (London, Dacre Press, 1945), p. 393.

will do for us. It is the place where we meet Christ the Savior. It is here, while waiting for the coming of the Kingdom, that we celebrate the marriage of Christ to His Bride. It is here that by communing with Christ we can commune with our brothers in the mystery of the Church. It is here that by receiving the Body and Blood of the Risen One we enter into the mystery of His Body and contemplate His Resurrection.

We will understand all this more clearly after studying the celebration itself in detail. However, it should now be clear to us that the eucharistic communion is a mystery of love which is lived rather than understood, and that it is far more important to participate in the eucharistic supper than to describe it.

CHAPTER 24

The Celebration of the Eucharist

Since that time soon after Pentecost when the disciples "devoted themselves to the apostles' teaching and fellowship, to the breaking of bread and the prayers" (Acts 2:42), the Church of Christ has never ceased to follow the teaching of the apostles and to break bread in brotherly communion every Sunday.[32] This is what we now call the Divine Liturgy.

Even though the celebration of the Liturgy assumes many different forms following local traditions, it has always conformed to the same basic pattern. According to all available evidence, this pattern dates back to apostolic tradition, that is, to the apostolic practice which is the common source of all local church traditions.[33] We will try to describe this apostolic tradition which forms the core of all the liturgies which have been used by Orthodox Christians from the beginning to the present. We will pay particular attention to the Liturgies of St John Chrysostom,[34] St Basil, [35] St James,[36] and St Mark.[37]

A) The Teaching of the Apostles: The Liturgy of the Word

St Justin (who was martyred in Rome c. 165 A.D.) tells us that

---

32. In Greek, Sunday is *kyriake,* from *kyrios,* Lord.

33. A local church is defined as the assembly of all Christians from a specific locale around a single bishop.

34. This is the one most frequently used. It has been used in Constantinople since the time that St John Chrysostom was bishop there.

35. Celebrated on all Sundays during Lent as well as the day before Christmas and Theophany, St Basil's day, January 1, Holy Thursday, and Holy Saturday. It was used by St Basil in Caesarea, Asia Minor.

36. The liturgy of the Church of Jerusalem, celebrated on St James' day, October 23.

37. The liturgy of the Alexandrian Church, which may be used by other Churches on St Mark's day, April 25.

the celebration of the eucharistic mystery was preceded by readings from the Bible, followed by comments and explanations given by the head of the congregation, the *proestos* or bishop. This is the part which we now call "the liturgy of the Word" or "the liturgy of the catechumens" (because those who came for baptismal instruction were permitted to attend).

The readings include:

1. Readings from the Old Testament. In the Liturgy of St John Chrysostom these include Psalms 102 [103] and 145 [146] which are sung. The Liturgy of St Basil, when celebrated with vespers, includes various readings which correspond to the feast.

2. The reading of the Epistle, that is, of a letter addressed by one of the apostles to one of their churches (for example, the Epistles of St Paul to the Romans, Corinthians, Thessalonians).

3. The reading of the Gospel, that is, of a passage from one of the Gospels according to Matthew, Mark, Luke, or John. This is the unique, "Gospel," the Good News, which the Lord Jesus brought to the world.

These readings are followed by an explanation or commentary by the head of the congregation (the bishop or, in his absence, the priest).

The procession which we call the "little" or "lesser entrance" takes place during this first part of the Liturgy. The deacon solemnly brings out the Gospel book, which is the "icon" of the Word of God. He processes into the midst of the faithful and then, followed by the other clergy, returns through the royal doors (the doors of heaven) into the sanctuary, the Kingdom of God.

This action reminds us of the work of the Son of God, the Word made flesh, who came into the world to enlighten mankind (Jn 1:9). He went out among the people to make Himself known and to help them to know the Father: "If you had known Me, you would have known My Father also" (Jn 14:7). In this way He will lead them into the Kingdom.

After the coming of the Word into the world has thus been represented, it is heard as the deacon reads the Gospel which he has just brought out. The memorial is transformed into reality. The com-

THE TABLE BELOW SUMMARIZES THE SCHEMA
OF THE LITURGY OF ST JOHN CHRYSOSTOM

I. Liturgy of the Word	1—Readings from the O.T. 2—Small Entrance 3—Reading of the Epistle 4—Reading of the Gospel 5—Preaching		
II. Liturgy of the Eucharist	1—"He took": Great Entrance Kiss of Peace—Creed		
	2—"He gave thanks" = Anaphora	A) Thanksgiving to the Father	a) for creation
			b) Trinitarian praise: Sanctus
			c) for redemption
		B) Memorial of the work of the Son	a) institution
			b) anamnesis
			c) anaphora
		C) Invocation for descent of the Holy Spirit D) Final doxology	a) epiclesis
			b) commemoration of the dead, hymn to the Theotokos
			c) commemoration of the living
	3—He "broke" Fraction	A) Lord's Prayer	
		B) Holy Things for the Holy	
		C) Fraction of the Bread	
	4—He "gave" Communion	A) "With the fear of God . . . draw near . . ."	
		B) "We have seen the true light	

memoration of the coming of the Word becomes the proclamation
of this Word, touching our hearts even today through the power of
the Holy Spirit. It is He who helps us to receive and understand the
Word of the Son. That is why the reading of the Gospel is preceded
by a prayer[38] in which we ask God to make His light shine in our

---

38. A true, short form of the epiclesis (an invocation to make the representation become
    reality).

hearts. Thus the Word becomes present among us. God speaks to His people in order to transform them into His Bride, His Church, and we listen to the Word with open heart and soul so that we may live by it. This is the purpose of the celebration.

B) The Celebration of the Mystery ("the Breaking of Bread"): the Liturgy of the Eucharist

The second part is also called the liturgy of the faithful because only baptized believers, the faithful, can participate in the great and awesome mystery which commemorates the Crucifixion and Resurrection of our Savior. Anyone coming simply as a spectator or a tourist would profane the love of Him who shed His Blood for the life of the world. That is why the deacon asks the catechumens (that is, those who are not yet baptized) to depart and the faithful to watch the doors, so that only the initiated stay at the celebration of the marriage of the Lamb to His faithful people.

The liturgy of the Eucharist is composed of four parts. These parts correspond to the four actions of Christ at the Last Supper on Holy Thursday and also to His action during His meeting with the two disciples on the road to Emmaus.[39]

1. He took bread.
2. He gave thanks.
3. He broke it.
4. He gave it to His Apostles and disciples.

In the liturgy of the Eucharist the four parts are:

1. The great entrance or offertory.
2. The anaphora or eucharistic prayer.
3. The breaking of the Bread.
4. Communion.

Let us now study these four great parts in greater detail:

39. See Part V, p. 211.

The Great Entrance

At this point the deacons and priests come out among the faithful carrying the paten,[40] which holds the bread, and the chalice, into which a mixture of wine and water has been poured. They present these to the bishop who stands before the royal doors. He takes them (just as Christ took the bread and the cup) and places them on the holy table as an offering to God.

This "ascent" of the clergy into the sanctuary, offering the bread and wine, the signs of the Body and Blood of Christ,[41] in the name of the people, represents the offering which Christ made of Himself when He ascended Golgotha and the Cross and, through the Cross, entered into His Kingdom. That is why at this moment we remember the words of the good thief on the cross, "Remember me, O Lord, when Thou comest in Thy Kingdom," and the priest adds, "May the Lord God remember you in His Kingdom always." All the faithful offer themselves "as a living sacrifice, holy and acceptable to God" (Rom 12:1), remembering the supreme sacrifice of their Master.

The Anaphora

This is the most important prayer of the Divine Liturgy. It is based on the prayer of thanksgiving (*eucharistia* in Greek) which Christ pronounced after taking the bread and cup. As we have seen, it originated in the thanksgiving, blessing, or *berakoth* of Israel (which the Jews continue to celebrate today, omitting the thanksgiving for the New Covenant which they do not yet accept).

This prayer is introduced by the exclamation, "Let us lift up our hearts," to which the people respond, "We lift them up unto the Lord." The celebrant then says, "Let us give thanks unto the Lord," and the people sing, "It is meet and right." This is followed by a long act of thanksgiving, a heartfelt "eucharist" which lends its name

---

40. The paten is a small plate, usually made of silver, on which the bread prepared for the offering (called the Lamb) is placed.
41. Signs: *antitypa* in Greek; in the Liturgy of St Basil, antitypes.

to the whole celebration. We all have a tendency to forget that the Divine Liturgy is fundamentally an act of thanksgiving. We have become so used to receiving gifts from our Creator that we no longer acknowledge our Benefactor and no longer express our gratitude to Him. We no longer know how to say, "Thank you, my God"; we no longer know how to celebrate a Eucharist.

Nevertheless, God's people express their gratitude to the heavenly Father through the Divine Liturgy, obeying the commandment the Lord gave shortly before His death. This commandment embodies His whole Testament, the New Testament: "Do this in remembrance of Me."

So let us study the prayer of the anaphora more closely. The Jewish meal was followed by three *berakoth* or benedictions. The first gave thanks for creation. The second gave thanks for the redemption, that is, for the liberation of the Jewish people from the tyranny of Pharaoh in the Exodus from Egypt. The third was a prayer asking for the coming of the Messiah and the Kingdom of God.

The Christian anaphora also has three parts which correspond exactly to the three *berakoth*. This shows that the source of our liturgical anaphora is the prayer of thanksgiving offered by Christ on Holy Thursday. However, it now takes on trinitarian characteristics.

The first part consists of a prayer of thanksgiving addressed to the Father, in which we thank Him for creation.

The second part is the grateful remembrance of the Son's act of redemption and liberation.

The third part consists of the supplication or invocation, the epiclesis, in which we ask for the descent of the Holy Spirit so that through Him we may receive "the fulfillment of the Kingdom of Heaven."

The head of the congregation (usually the bishop or, in his absence, the senior priest) pronounces the prayer of the anaphora on behalf of the people.

The First Part: A Prayer of Thanksgiving Addressed to the Father

1) The celebrant gives thanks to God for all creation

He thanks God for having created us, for "Thou it was who brought us from non-existence into being." The beginning of faith is to recognize that our existence has its source in God's act of creation and to thank Him for it. "By faith we understand that the world was created by the word of God, so that what is seen was made out of things which do not appear" (Heb 11:3). This is gratitude at its most elementary level.

2) The celebrant sings praise to the living God: the singing of the Sanctus

Our gratitude to God is expressed in praise. We praise the God who does wonders, the true God, the living God, the God of the Trinity, the thrice-holy God, the One whose praise is sung without ceasing by the angels. That is why our prayer of thanksgiving is followed by the triumphal hymn, first heard in 740 B.C. by the prophet Isaiah in the temple in Jerusalem (Is 6:3) and heard again for the second time by St John on Patmos (Rev 4:8): "Holy! Holy! Holy! Lord of Saboath![42] Heaven and earth are full of Thy glory." The song of the celestial hosts, the archangels and angels, seraphim and cherubim, is repeated at every Liturgy by the people as they sing the Sanctus. The song of the angels is followed by the song of the children of Jerusalem as they greeted Christ the King coming into His capital on Palm Sunday: "Blessed is He that comes in the name of the Lord! Hosannah in the highest!

3) The celebrant gives thanks for the work of redemption

We have thanked the Father for creation; we must also thank Him

---

42. Sabaoth is a Hebrew word meaning the Lord of hosts. It undoubtedly refers to angelic armies.

for giving His only Son, who will deliver us from the Fall and from death. This prayer of thanksgiving to the Father leads into the second part of the anaphora.

The Second Part: The Remembrance of Christ's Work

This is the supreme act of thanksgiving of the New Covenant. It is a commemoration of everything that the Son of God did for us, beginning with His actions on the eve of His Death at the Last Supper. It is an account of the institution of the Eucharist. It recapitulates Jesus' words, "Take! Eat! This is My Body which is broken for you, for the remission of sins," and then "Drink of it, all of you! This is My Blood of the New Testament, which is shed for you and for many, for the remission of sins!"

To obey the command to "do this in remembrance of Me," we "make anamnesis"[43]: we commemorate

His Death

His Resurrection

His Ascension

His Sitting at the right hand of the Father

His second and glorious Coming—

in short everything that He has done, is doing, and will do for us. This is a commemoration of the Son's eternal action which transcends time and brings together the past, present, and future. Taking a Greek word, used by St Paul in 1 Cor 11:25, we call this the *anamnesis*.

The Anaphora

This commemoration is not simply an intellectual act: Jesus said, "Do this in remembrance of Me." What did He actually do? He took bread and wine representing the sacrifice which He was about to make of His Body and Blood on the Cross and offered them to God.

---

43. *Anamnesis* is a Greek word meaning remembrance, memorial, an act which makes a past event real by reminding not only us but also God of its occurence.

In obedience to Christ's commandment and in gratitude for His sacrifice, the celebrant now offers the bread and wine to God: "Thine own of Thine own we offer unto Thee." This is the anaphora (in Greek *anaphora* means offering, or "lifting up"). It is the supreme offering of the Church, an offering of the antitypes (as the Liturgy of St Basil says), the signs of Christ's Body and Blood in the form of bread and wine, in remembrance of His supreme sacrifice. The offerings and sacrifices of the Old Testament were bloody, involving the slaughter of animals; the offering and sacrifice of the New Testament is "reasonable and bloodless." It consists of bread and wine which represent the actual offering, that is, Christ's sacrifice on the Cross.

And even though the bishop offers the paten and chalice to God the Father with crossed and outstretched arms, it is the people, the Church as a whole, who give thanks to God for the sacrifice of His Son.

The Third Part: The Supplication for the Descent of the Holy Spirit

1) The Epiclesis

In the third part of the anaphora, the Holy Spirit comes to complete and seal the great trinitarian mystery enacted in the Eucharist. It would be useless to commemorate Christ's sacrifice if we did not obey His command, "Take! Eat! This is My Body which is broken for you, for the remission of sins . . . Drink of it, all of you! This is My Blood of the New Testament, which is shed for you and for many, for the remission of sins." For it is not bread which is broken for the remission of sins, nor wine which is spilled by Christ; it is His most precious Body and Blood. "[U]nless you eat the flesh of the Son of man and drink His blood, you have no life in you; he who eats My flesh and drinks My blood has eternal life, and I will raise him up at the last day" (Jn 6:53-54). Thus the bread and wine which is offered by the Church must become the Body and Blood offered by Christ. The words, "This is My Body . . . This is My Blood," must be confirmed by Him who will "bring to your remembrance all that I have said to you" (Jn 14:26), who "will take what is Mine and declare it to you" (Jn 16:14), who "confirmed the message by the signs that attended it" (Mk 16:20). The Holy Spirit must make the words pronounced by Christ on Holy Thursday real and actual today. The bread must actually become the Body of Christ and the wine must actually become the Blood of Christ. For this to happen the Church's offering must be consumed by a heavenly Fire just as the sacrifice of the great prophet Elijah had been.[44] Then it is truly transformed into the sacrifice which the Risen Lamb offers to the Father for the remission of sins. The Risen One must be made present through Pentecost. The Holy Spirit who hovered over the waters so that the word of the Creator was fulfilled (Gen 1:2), the Spirit who made the Word dwell in Mary's womb on the day of the Annunciation and in the bosom of the Church at Pentecost, must now make Christ's sacrifice real in the midst of today's eucharistic assembly. It is the presence of the Word which transforms this assembly into the Church, the Body of Christ. That is why the celebrant addresses God the Father on behalf of the congregation, saying, "[We] ask Thee, and pray Thee, and supplicate Thee: Send down Thy Holy Spirit upon us and upon these Gifts here offered. And make this Bread the precious Body of Thy Christ"; the people answer, "Amen." "And that which is in this Cup, the precious Blood of Thy Christ"; "Amen." "Making the change by Thy Holy Spirit"; "Amen, amen, amen." "That they may be to those who partake for the purification of soul, for the remission of sins, for the communion of Thy Holy Spirit, for the fulfillment of the Kingdom of Heaven . . ."

This prayer is called the epiclesis. We must understand that in it the Holy Spirit is not only called down upon us but also upon these Gifts, that is, the bread and wine. Material things too are open to the action of the Holy Spirit. Communion with bread and wine would be meaningless if these Gifts had not been transformed into Christ's Body and Blood by the Holy Spirit. However, we pray for the descent of the Holy Spirit upon the Gifts so that we too may be transformed.

---

44. See Part III, chapter 6.

We ask the Holy Spirit to change the bread and wine so that through them we may receive "remission of sins," discover "the communion of Thy Holy Spirit," and taste "the fulfillment of the Kingdom" in this world. The Holy Spirit touches us through the gifts. That is why, in the epiclesis of St Basil's Liturgy, we ask that the Holy Spirit "unite all of us to one another who become partakers of the one Bread and Cup in the communion of the Holy Spirit." As soon as we are united to one another in the communion of the Holy Spirit, we become the Church just as the disciples did on Pentecost. The epiclesis is a continuing Pentecost.

2) The Sanctification of the Dead

The unity realized through the power of the Holy Spirit includes the faithful of all generations and countries. That is why the epiclesis is followed by a prayer for the dead, "for those who have fallen asleep in the faith: ancestors, fathers, patriarchs, prophets, apostles, preachers, evangelists, martyrs, confessors, ascetics, and every righteous spirit made perfect in faith. Especially for our most holy, most pure, most blessed and glorious Lady Theotokos and ever-virgin Mary." This is the sanctification of the dead, followed by a hymn to the Virgin.

3) The Sanctification of the Living

We also pray for "the episcopate . . . and every order of the clergy . . . travelers . . . the sick . . . captives . . . those who bring offerings and do good . . ." This is the sanctification of the living. The whole Church, earthly and celestial, is united in faith and the communion of the Holy Spirit through the mystery of the Eucharist.

The Church unites mankind and the heavenly powers, saints and sinners, the living and the dead, for all are alive in Christ. "[W]e, though many, are one body in Christ, and individually members one of another" (Rom 12:5), St Paul teaches us. We are all responsible for each other and that is how we survive, for the angels intercede on our behalf. This unity of all in the Body of Christ is called the communion of the saints.

It is only natural that this magnificent discovery of the communion of the saints should be followed by a song of praise, a doxology[45] which concludes the anaphora. "And grant that with one mouth and one heart we may praise Thine all-honorable and majestic name: of the Father, and of the Son, and of the Holy Spirit, now and ever and unto ages of ages. Amen."

"He Broke": the Breaking of the Bread

Before the celebrant breaks the Bread in imitation of Christ's action, the faithful proclaim their brotherly unity by reciting or singing together the Lord's Prayer, the "Our Father." In this way, as children of the same Father, we prepare to share the same bread. Reciting the Lord's Prayer in preparation for Communion is a universal and permanent element in Christian tradition.

In the breaking of the Bread, the celebrant lifts it up saying, "The Holy things for the holy." He uses the word "the holy" in the same way that St Paul so often did, to designate the faithful. For we are all called to become saints, to be made holy by the same Holy Spirit who has just sanctified the Gifts. The faithful respond, protesting that they are not saints: "One is Holy. One is the Lord, Jesus Christ, to the glory of God the Father. Amen." He is the only source of holiness.

The celebrant then breaks the Bread and puts the pieces or fragments into a single Cup so that all the faithful can communicate of the same Body and Blood of the only Lord. The fact that the same Bread and the same Cup will be shared by all demonstrates the unity of the Church achieved through communion with the one Lord. This is the importance of the act of breaking and sharing performed by the Lord Jesus Christ Himself.

---

45. A doxology is the act of rendering praise; from the Greek *doxa*, glory, and *logos*, word.

The Eucharist: Distribution of the Bread

"He gave": the Communion

This is the climax, the purpose of the whole celebration. The guests
at the wedding feast, the heavenly banquet, the mystical supper,
approach the holy table "in the fear of God, with faith and love."
They step up to the royal doors (in the Coptic Church they even enter
the sanctuary). They go to meet the divine Bridegroom who greets
them at the entrance into the bridal chamber. They are about to be
made one with His resurrected Body. His life-giving Blood will flow
through their veins. They will all be united in His Body; they will
all drink from the Fountain of Life, for the Lord said, "Drink, all
of you." God made flesh will divinize their flesh. The immaterial
Fire, which burned but did not consume the bush on Sinai and which
descended in the form of tongues upon the assembly of the apostles,
the Fire which has just transformed the Bread and Wine, will spread
and inflame the hearts and bodies of the communicants. In response,
they will sing: "We have seen the true Light! We have received the

The Eucharist: Distribution of the Wine

heavenly Spirit! We have found the true Faith! Worshipping the undivided Trinity, who has saved us."

The congregation has become the Church. God is in the midst of His people, and they contemplate with wonder the Resurrection of their Lord:

> Having beheld the Resurrection of Christ, let us worship the holy Lord Jesus, the only Sinless One. We venerate Thy Cross, O Christ, and we praise and glorify Thy holy Resurrection; for Thou art our God, and we know no other than Thee; we call on Thy name. Come all you faithful, let us venerate Christ's holy Resurrection! For, behold, through the Cross joy has come into all the world. Let us ever bless the Lord, praising His Resurrection, for by enduring the Cross for us, He has destroyed death by death.

The congregation has become a congregation of the truly living. They can depart in peace and proclaim the Resurrection of their Lord to the whole world in the joyful expectation of His Second Coming.

We Have Seen the True Light

Kievan Chant

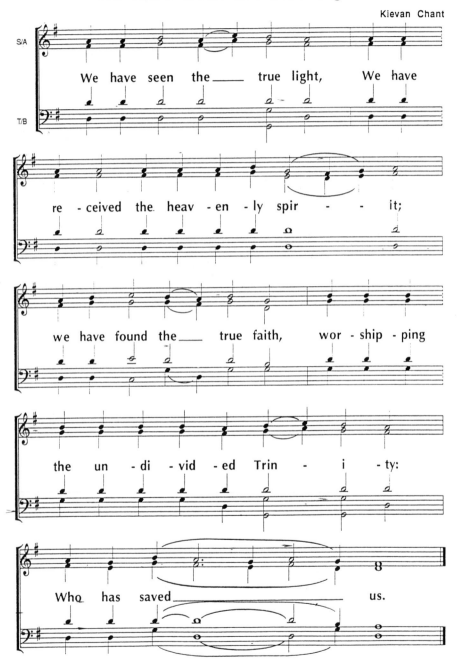

We have seen the ___ true light, We have re-ceived the heav-en-ly spir - - it; we have found the ___ true faith, wor - ship - ping the un - di - vid - ed Trin - i - ty: Who has saved ___ us.

CHAPTER 25

THE MYSTERY AND PRIESTHOOD OF CHRIST AND OF THE CHURCH

A) The Mystery of Christ; the Mystery of the Church

Those who communicate of the Body and Blood of the Risen Lord can catch a glimpse of what St Paul calls the mystery of Christ in his Epistle to the Colossians (4:3): "the mystery hidden for ages and generations but now made manifest in His saints" (Col 1:26).

We cannot attempt to "understand" this mystery, for it is infinitely greater and deeper than human intelligence, which is able to understand or comprehend[46] only something lesser than itself. Rather we must contemplate it with wonder as St Paul did when he encountered it on the road to Damascus.

1. Christ, the Son of Mary, is a man like us. Everything that is in Him is communicable to other people. That is why He can save us.

2. Christ, the only Son of God, is God, the same God as His Father and His Holy Spirit. That is why He can unite us to the Father.

3. Through communion with the Body and Blood of Christ we are incorporated into His resurrected Body. We become one Body with Him and participants in His divinity. This mysterious Body created by the union of the Head (Christ) with the members (the communicants) is called the Church.

4. The head of a body controls the members, making them move. In the same way, Christ acts as the moving force in relation to the faithful, the members of His Church. Through His Church Christ is present and active in the world. The members of the Church respond to the impulses sent by the Head, listening to His Word.

46. Comprehend is derived from the Latin *comprehendere,* to contain.

5. The parts of a body can live only if the blood which comes from the heart flows through them. Members of the Church can be living members only if the Holy Spirit circulates through them, uniting them to each other and to the Head.

6. The mystery of the Church consists in the fact that sinful but believing people are united to the Body of the risen Christ through the action of the Holy Spirit. They become members of the single Body, Christ, and carry on His work in today's world, for He speaks and acts through them.

7. This mystery of Christ, or of the Church, has many aspects, which St Paul calls "the mysteries of God" (1 Cor 4:1), and which Orthodox Christians usually call simply "mysteries." In Latin they are called *sacramenta,* hence the English world "sacrament."[47]

B) The Priesthood of Christ; the Priesthood of the Church

The Priesthood of Christ

The Lord Jesus, being both God and man, reestablished communication between divinity and humanity. He makes us hear God's voice, for He is the Word of God made flesh. Having ascended into heaven in His human nature, He has become our advocate before God the Father, appearing "in the presence of God on our behalf" and presenting Him with a sacrifice "once for all when He offered up Himself" for His brothers and sisters (Heb 9:24; 7:27). This function as intermediary between God and man is called "the priesthood of Christ." Because of this sacerdotal function,[48] Christ is given the title of High Priest in the Epistle to the Hebrews and in all Christian tradition. Psalm 109 [110], cited in the Epistle to the Hebrews (7:21) states, "Thou art a priest forever."

47. We suggest that those who would like to meditate more deeply upon this "mystery of Christ" reread the following passages: Rom 12:2-6a; 1 Cor 12:4-7; 15; Eph 1:9-10; 2:19-22; Col 1:26-27; 4:3.

48. From the Latin word *sacerdos,* meaning minister of the sacred, priest; the equivalent in Greek is *hiereus.* We must always make a distinction between *hiereus,* the minister of the sacred, the one who sacrifices, and *presbyteros,* meaning elder, the one responsible for the community. Unfortunately both of these Greek words are rendered in English as "priest," which therefore takes on both meanings.

The Priesthood of the Church

Christ is thus our High Priest. As we have seen, He acts in the world through His Body, the Church; it is through her that His voice is heard. He makes her a partner in the sacrifice of His own Body which He offers to the Father. Christ does nothing without His Body; the Church participates fully in Christ's priesthood. This means that the Lord Jesus asks for our collaboration in carrying out His work in the world and in addressing His Father. St Paul tells us, "we are God's fellow workers" (1 Cor 3:9). When a Christian leans lovingly over someone who is suffering, he acts as the hand of Christ; when he declares the truth of the Gospel, he acts as Christ's mouth. But he must first become a true member of Christ's Body through the power of the Holy Spirit. The Holy Spirit must make him a "priest," that is, a person who participates in Christ's work, in Christ's priesthood. This change is effected through what we call the Mystery of Chrismation.

CHAPTER 26

THE MYSTERY OF CHRISMATION:
THE PERSONAL PENTECOST
OR
THE ROYAL PRIESTHOOD OF THE LAITY

"The Spirit was given through the laying on of the apostles' hands," St Luke tells us in Acts 8:18. He gives us two examples of this.

A) Acts 8:4-25

The first great persecution of the Christian Church occurred in about 36 A.D. after the stoning of Stephen. The Christians of Jerusalem were dispersed, fleeing this persecution, and the deacon Philip went to Samaria, preaching Christ as he went. The Samaritans accepted the Word of God, but "they had only been baptized in the name of the Lord Jesus" and the Holy Spirit "had not yet fallen on any of them" (Acts 8:16). "[T]he apostles at Jerusalem . . . sent to them Peter and John, who came down and prayed for them that they might receive the Holy Spirit . . . Then they laid their hands on them and they received the Holy Spirit" (Acts 8:14, 15, 17).

B) Acts 19:1-7

Something similar happened when St Paul went to Ephesus in about 56 A.D.

> There he found some disciples. And he said to them "Did you receive the Holy Spirit when you believed?" And they said, "No, we have never even heard that there is a Holy Spirit." And he said, "Into what then were you baptized?" They said, "Into John's bap-

tism." And Paul said, "John baptized with the baptism of repentance, telling the people to believe in the One who was to come after him, that is, Jesus." On hearing this, they were baptized in the name of the Lord Jesus. And when Paul had laid his hands upon them, the Holy Spirit came upon them,[49] and they spoke with tongues and prophesied. (Acts 19:1-6)

Thus these new disciples received the Holy Spirit through the laying on of hands, just as the apostles had received Him on Pentecost at Jerusalem. The gift of Pentecost was present in the past and continues to be present today. This is what we call the Mystery of Chrismation, from the Greek word *chrisma,* which means "unction." This is the unction of the Holy Spirit, through which we become what Christ has always been: "anointed ones" of the Holy Spirit, little christs, Christians.

Today this mystery is usually celebrated immediately after Baptism.[50] The newly baptized is anointed with oil just as King David was at his chrismation.[51]

In his First Epistle, St John says, "You have been anointed" (1 Jn 2:20), and the apostle Paul says, "He has put His seal upon us and given us His Spirit in our hearts" (2 Cor 1:22).

The apostle Peter evokes the sacred character of this unction conferred on God's people in a particularly striking manner: "You are a chosen race, a royal priesthood, a holy nation" (1 Pet 2:9).

Seeker: What does "a royal priesthood, a holy nation" mean?

Sage: We have seen that Christ is our High Priest, that is, the intermediary between God and us; that He is God's spokesman and our advocate before God, and that this wonderful role is called priesthood. We have also seen that He makes His whole Body, the entire

---

49. Notice the connection between baptism in the name of the Lord Jesus and the descent of the Holy Spirit; as soon as we meet Christ we are led to receive the Holy Spirit who rests upon Him, and the Spirit in turn makes us exclaim, "Abba, Father." A Christian cannot think of one Person of the Trinity without thinking of the other two. The only true God, the living God, is the God in three Persons.

50. See Part V, p. 227.

51. Roman Catholics celebrate this mystery through the imposition of hands by a bishop. It is called "Confirmation."

Church and all its members, a part of this priesthood. But the
members of the Church must first be clothed in His sanctity. His
priestly function must be transferred to them; they must become
priests, inheritors of His Kingdom and future kings. St John tells
us in Revelation that "[He] made us a kingdom, priests to His God"
(Rev 1:6; 5:10). The Church is a nation of priests; Chrismation
transforms every Christian into a priest. This is what we now call
"the royal priesthood of the laity" through which Christians become
a priestly and royal community.

Seeker: I thought that "layman" meant "stranger to the Church."
In fact, the dictionary says that a layman is "someone who is neither
an ecclesiastic nor a monastic."

Sage: Words often change their meaning with the evolution of
ideas and historical events. "Layman" is derived from the Greek word
laos, which means people. Thus it meant originally, and still means
to Christians today, "members of God's nations." It is only when
Christians ceased being real Christians and forgot that they were a
nation of priests and kings that the word took on the meaning you
found in the dictionary. It is high time for Christians to rediscover
the sacred, priestly character of their lay condition. The assembly of
Christians bears the permanent responsibility of being the earthly
representatives of Christ's royalty and priesthood: through their
participation in the divine Eucharist; through the love which should
reign among them; through their kindness to their enemies; through
their firmness in rejecting the selfish compromises in which the
wicked of this world seek to embroil them; through the whole witness
of this community to believer-communicants. They are truly a
priestly and royal community (in Greek, *basilein hierateuma*).

Through Chrismation each one of us receives the Holy Spirit, a
Gift which makes us members of this priestly nation. This Gift is
the source of all other gifts of the Spirit, which confer a specific
responsibility. Thus the role of bishop, priest, and deacon is simply
a functional differentiation of this fundamental Gift.

CHAPTER 27

THE ORDINATION OF BISHOPS, PRIESTS AND DEACONS, OR THE PRIESTLY MINISTRY

A) The Bishop and the Councils

The Bishop

In his first letter to Timothy, St Paul says, "Do not neglect the gift you have, which was given you by prophetic utterance when the council of elders laid their hands upon you" (1 Tim 4:14).[52] And in a second letter he says, "I remind you to rekindle the gift of God that is within you through the laying on of my hands" (2 Tim 1:6).[53]

He also tells Timothy to ordain elders ("Do not be hasty in the laying on of hands," [1 Tim 5:22] and entrust them with the apostolic teaching: "And what you have heard from me before many witnesses entrust to faithful men who will be able to teach others also" (2 Tim 2:2). He asks Timothy to "remain at Ephesus" (1 Tim 1:3) to carry out this mission.

Thus, in the person of Timothy we have a living example of what the generation which followed the apostles, the "Apostolic Fathers," will call a bishop.

Seeker: What is a bishop?
Sage: He is the one who presides over the eucharistic assembly, as St Justin, who died c. 165 A.D., tells us. As a result he discharges three functions in the city where he lives;

---

52. Elders: *Presbyteroi* in Greek, from which our word priest is derived.
53. "The laying on of hands": apparently Timothy was ordained by the simultaneous laying on of hands by the apostle Paul and the assembly of priests *(presbyteroi).*

a) He is charged with leading the people of God toward the King-dom just as Moses led them into the Promised Land.

b) He must nurture them with the true word ("What you have heard from me entrust to faithful men who will be able to teach others also"). He must transmit to them the teaching which the apostles received from Christ. This transmission of Christ's truth, of which the bishops are guardians, is what we call the "apostolic tradition." And the uninterrupted succession of bishops is called the "apostolic succession." It guarantees the unity of the Church through the ages, linking successive generation by proclaiming the same truth, the same Word of God.

c) The bishop is charged with feeding the people of God with the heavenly Bread which the priests distribute at the eucharistic assem-bly over which he presides.[54] The presence of a successor to the apostles at the head of the eucharistic assembly shows that this assembly was indeed founded by Christ and His apostles; that it is part of the one, holy, catholic, and apostolic Church. The bishop who brings together the faithful of his own district to partake of the Body and Blood of Christ must himself be in communion with the bishops of other districts. He is the link between his own church and all others. He is a guarantee of the Church's unity in geographic space.

Thus the bishop plays an esential role in articulating the Body of Christ; he insures its unity through time and space. that is why St Ignatius of Antioch[55] tells us, "Where the bishop is, there also is the catholic Church."[56]

Thus the college of bishops has the same function in the Church as the college of the twelve apostles had. It guarantees the "aposto-

54. That is why the bishop is always prayed for at the Liturgy, reminding us of his presence, even if he is physically elsewhere.
55. The bishop of that city. He wrote this often-quoted sentence in a letter to the Church at Smyrna, where St Polycarp was bishop, while on his way to Rome where he was martyred.
56. Catholic is from the Greek word *kat'holon,* meaning the whole, totality. If its members are Othodox, the Church is called catholic because it is identified with the totality of Christ's Body. That is why in the Creed we say, "I believe in one, holy, catholic, and apostolic Church." In popular usage since the schism, the word "Catholic" is used to refer to the Roman Catholic Church, while "Orthodox" refers to those Churches which have preserved the orthodox faith.

licity" of the Church, that is, the continuity of its life and teaching from the time of the apostles themselves.

Councils

Councils are assemblies of bishops. There are several kinds of councils: regional councils should meet twice yearly; national councils meet every three years. In exceptional circumstances an international council may be called; this is an ecumenical council. Only seven councils have been recognized by the Church as truly ecumenical.[57] However, whenever a false doctrine arose to trouble the conscience of the faithful or to distort the image of Christ which the Church must present to the world, in other words, whenever the Church's Body required it, local councils[58] were called. Through these councils the Church was able to express the truth which she embodies.

57. Here are the places and dates of the seven ecumenical councils:
    1st—Nicaea, 325.
    2nd—Constaninople, 381.
    3rd—Ephesus, 431.
    4th—Chalcedon, 451.
    5th—Constantinople, 553.
    6th—Constantinople, 680-81
    7th—Nicaea, 787.
58. Here are four examples of local councils.
    a) When the reality of the Church's experience of the Light of the Holy Spirit was contested in the fourteenth century, the so-called "Palamite" councils were assembled in Constantinople in 1341, 1347, and 1351. They confirmed the orthodoxy of St Gregory Palamas' teaching.
    b) When, in the seventeenth century, Calvin's ideas were introduced into the Orthodox Church by Cyril Lukaris, Patriarch of Constantinople, a whole series of local councils were assembled from 1638 to 1691 in Constantinople, in Jassy (Moldavia, present day Rumania) in 1643, and in Jerusalem in 1662, to define Orthodox teaching in relation to Protestantism.
    c) When Pope Pius IX tried to force the Orthodox to recognize the supremacy of the Roman papacy in an encyclical addressed to the "Oriental Churches," the Eastern patriarchs assembled synods and consulted one another. The result was a common encyclical entitled, "Encyclical Epistle of the One, Holy, Catholic, and Apostolic Church to the Orthodox of the Whole World." Dated May 1848, it defined the Orthodox position in relation to the Roman claims. (These claims culminated twenty years later in the proclamation of the dogma of papal infallibility.)

The mission of the councils is to manifest "the union of God's holy churches" by expressing the unity and orthodoxy[59] of the faith of the catholic Church, so that Christians in all places and at all times may believe what Christ and the apostles taught. The councils are not a form of government. The unity of the church is maintained through faith, love, and a common vision inspired by the Holy Spirit. When the Holy Spirit enlightens the conscience of all, He creates what we call "the communion of the Holy Spirit."

The community of churches from a given region, assembled around the bishops of this region, is called "the local church."[60] All local churches should maintain harmonious relations with each other. The Church of Rome had been entrusted with the duty of "presiding in love" among them, as St Ignatius of Antioch tells us. However, since there has been a break between the Church of Rome on the one hand and the Churches of Constantinople, Alexandria, Antioch and Jerusalem on the other,[61] it is the Church of Constantinople,

---

d) When, in the nineteenth century, an overzealous nationalism led the Bulgarians to refuse to accept Greek bishops, a council was called in Constantinople in 1872. It condemned "phyletism," a heresy in which more importance is given to the national ideal than to the unity of faith.

59. Orthodoxy: according to Greek etymology *orthos* means right and *doxa* mean opinion, judgment, esteem, or glory.

In current usage the word orthodox describes someone who follows to the letter the doctrine of the group to which he belongs.

The Fathers used the word "Orthodoxy' to designate the Church. To them it meant praise in Truth. For us, Orthodoxy means the True Faith.

60. In the strictly traditional sense, a local church is the eucharistic community assembled around a bishop in a specific geographic location. As we have seen above, the bishop guarantees the adherence of this church to the fullness of the apostolic faith. The consecration of the bishop by two or three other bishops is the visible sign that other local churches recognize his apostolic faith. They also recognize the apostolic faith of his church which becomes the apostolic Church of that particular region (cf. St Ignatius, "Where the bishop is, there is the catholic Church").

It is only by extension that we can apply the term "local church" to a community of many dioceses whose bishops meet at regional synods. Metropolias (made up of many dioceses) and patriarchates (made up of many dioceses and metropolias) developed historically to allow the more efficient practice of conciliarity. But the basic unit of a local church is the diocese which embodies the fullness of the church in a particular locality, on condition, of course, that it is in communion with the other churches.

61. We cite only the principal churches at the time of the schism.

"New Rome," which has assumed this role, in anticipation of the day when a return to the orthodox faith will allow the Roman Church to resume its rightful place in the community of churches.[62]

B) Priests

The English word priest is a shortened form of the Greek word *presbyteros,* or presbyter, meaning elder. In fact, the priests of the early Christian community were a continuation of the tradition of "elders" who presided over the Jewish communities. Even though they are leaders of a "priestly people" made holy by the Spirit, a priestly nation, a community of priests in the sense of *hiereus,* Christian priests participate in a particularly active way in the ministry and priesthood of Christ. Thus, if we compare the bishops' role to that of Moses as he led the children of Israel across the desert to the Promised Land, priests can be compared to the seventy-two elders of whom God said to Moses, "I will take some of the spirit which is upon you and put it upon them; and they shall bear the burden of the people with you, that you may not bear it yourself alone" (Num 11:17).

Under the unifying supervision of the bishop, priests carry on functions which are more or less similar to his but on a level at which they can maintain a personal contact with each one of the faithful. They can bring the Word of God and the consoling, forgiving, and healing presence of God's Spirit to each of the sheep whom the Lord loves. Thus, in accusing bad shepherds, the prophet Ezekiel says, "The weak you have not strengthened, the sick you have not healed, the crippled you have not bound up, the strayed you have not brought back, the lost you have not sought . . . So they were scattered, because there was no shepherd; and they became food for all the wild beasts" (Ezek 34:4-5). That is why the Lord Jesus is the Good Shepherd:

---

62. Since Vatican II the Roman Church has been trying to rediscover the local church in the fullness of its catholicity (the idea of sister churches). The role of the Roman Church and its bishops is defined in terms of a primacy of love and not simply of jurisdiction in the strict sense. But we are still far from achieving a true harmony of Churches.

Christ in Glory (John 20:19-23)

And Jesus went about all the cities and villages, teaching in their synagogues and preaching the Gospel of the Kingdom, and healing every disease and every infirmity. When He saw the crowds, He had compassion for them, because they were harassed and helpless, like sheep without a shepherd. Then He said to His disciples, "The harvest is plentiful, but the laborers are few; pray therefore the Lord of the harvest to send out laborers into His harvest." (Mt 9:35-37)

Chosen from among the people, celibate or married men (Ti 1:5-9),[63] priests are workers who remind all those who suffer that the Lord Jesus tells them:

Come to Me, all who labor and are heavy laden, and I will give you rest. Take My yoke upon you, and learn from Me; for I am gentle and lowly in heart, and you will find rest for your souls. For my yoke is easy, and My burden is light. (Mt 11:28-30).

C) Deacons

This word is derived from the Greek word *diakonos,* which means servant. The deacon is called upon to continue the service of the Servant Jesus, who washed the feet of His disciples, the "Suffering Servant" of whom Isaiah says, "The righteous one, My servant, [shall] make many to be accounted righteous" (Is 53:11).

In the beginning the deacons were given the task of serving tables at communal meals (Acts 6:2-3), because certain "widows were neglected in the daily distribution" (Acts 6:1). The apostles were then free to devote themselves to "prayer and to the ministry of the Word" (Acts 6:4).

The deacons' wonderful mission is, therefore, to serve the poor and also to serve at the eucharistic table: to distribute both earthly nourishment and heavenly bread to the faithful.

---

63. The Orthodox Church permits married men to be ordained. However, they are allowed to be married only once, and that before their ordination. The Latin Church changed this practice and imposed celibacy on all its priests only in the tenth century, during the papacy of Gregory V.

CHAPTER 28

THE SANCTIFICATION OF MARRIAGE

A body is made up of cells. In order for a body to live, the cells must also be living. For the Body of Christ to be alive, the Holy Spirit must constantly add new cells to it. He does this by transforming families into the cells of Christ's body, into cells of the Church. This is the mystery of the crowning, the consecration and sanctification of conjugal love by the Holy Spirit which is commonly called "the sacrament of Marriage."

The celebration of Marriage contains the same elements as the sacraments of Baptism[64] and the Eucharist,[65] that is:

1. The Offering.

2. A memorial or anamnesis in which the miracles performed by God for married couples are recalled with gratitude.

3. The epiclesis or invocation in which the Holy Spirit is asked to effect the same miracles on this particular occasion.

4. The communion, or the couple's participation in the life of the Kingdom.

A) The Offering

During the Eucharist the Church offers God bread and wine; during the celebration of a marriage the Church makes an offering of the bride and bridegroom, who in turn offer themselves to one another and to God. This is expressed in the promise to be faithful which the betrothed make to each other and to the congregation during the sevice of betrothal at which they receive the wedding rings as a token of fidelity.

64. See Part V, p. 312.
65. See Part VI, chapter 24.

B) The Anamnesis

In the Eucharist the anamnesis consists of a grateful evocation of Christ's whole work of salvation. In the celebration of marriage the anamnesis is a recital of all that God did for those holy couples who, from Abraham and Sarah to Joachim and Anna, made possible the birth of the Virgin Mary and, through her, of the Son of God.

It is also an evocation of Christ's marriage to the Church which is the mystical model for the union of man and woman. Finally, it recounts the story of the marriage of Cana in Galilee, at which Christ performed His first miracle. At His mother's request He changed colorless and flavorless water into hearty red wine—"good wine," the steward of the feast declared—thus bringing joy to the feast and transforming everything by His miraculous presence (Jn 2:1-11). God became flesh in order to transform our world, to sanctify our earthly life and to participate in our daily tasks.

C) The Epiclesis

In the Liturgy, the epiclesis is a prayer through which we ask God to send His Holy Spirit down upon the bread and wine to transform them into the Body and Blood of Christ.

In the sacrament of Marriage the epiclesis is the prayer through which we ask God to send His Holy Spirit down upon the man and woman, to "crown them with glory and honor" (at this point the priest holds crowns above their heads), to transform them into a living cell of Christ's Body. The Holy Spirit comes down to crown their love by His presence, to link their love to the source of all love, that is, to God Himself, "for God is love."

The couple will also be able to express man's likeness to God, for God created man in His image and likeness, "male and female He created them" (Gen 1:27). He created them so that the two, united by love, might become one flesh; just as Three are One in the divine model. In this way the Holy Spirit will help the man and woman to gradually transform themselves into the image of God. They will become their true selves only to the extent that they communicate with one another and become one, while still remaining two.

After the couple is crowned there is an explosion of joy, expressed in a kind of joyful dance around the Gospel book which represents the presence of Christ. At this moment we call upon Isaiah and the holy martyrs:

a) Isaiah, so that he may rejoice in the fulfillment of his prophecy; for he wrote, "Behold a Virgin shall conceive and bear a Son, and shall call His name Emmanuel," that is, God with us (Is 7:14). The newly crowned and sanctified couple also receive Emmanuel. The Word of God is now present within them; He is made incarnate in them. Thus, the couple becomes a miniature Church, a living cell in Christ's Body.

b) The holy martyrs—"who fought the good fight and have received your crowns"—are asked to help the newlyweds wage a good fight also so that in the end they too may attain a crown of glory. Married life is not easy. It involves a hard struggle, a total rejection of egotism, and the joyful acceptance of the Cross. It is an ascetic exercise through which one dies to oneself so that each may live for the other. "O Lord our God, . . . let that gladness come upon them which the blessed Helen had when she found the precious Cross." We are not ironical in comparing marriage to a glorious martyrdom.

D) The Communion

Like the Eucharist, marriage culminated in communion. The man and woman united by the Holy Spirit are now united in Christ. Together they become members of Christ's Body through eucharistic Communion. The rite of marriage included Communion with pre-sanctified Gifts[66] until the fifteenth century.[67]

The cup of wine, from which the bride and bridegroom drink together after reciting the Lord's Prayer, is a relic of this ancient practice. By taking communion together every Sunday, a couple ful-

---

66. This is Bread and Wine which were consecrated and sanctified during an earlier Liturgy and have been set aside for special use.

67. See John Meyendorff, *Marriage, An Orthodox Perspective*, 2nd ed., (Crestwood, NY, St. Vladimir's Seminary Press, 1975), pp. 30-31.

fills the true purpose of marriage: to enter together, as a family, into the mystery of Christ.

Let us not forget that love is creative and that the union of man and woman usually results in the procreation of children as a result of the couple's love for each other. The procreation of children is a divine blessing ardently prayed for during the marriage service and should be a goal for the married couple. The sacrament of Marriage is the foundation of a family church whose members, the couple and their children, approach the blessed Kingdom of Christ together.

The Holy Spirit sanctifies conjugal love through the sacrament of Marriage. However, let us not forget that since the time that John the Baptist retired into the desert to be alone with God, and since St Anthony the Great followed his example some three hundred years later in Egypt, a strong yearning for God has never ceased to inspire some people to seek union with the Love of God through solitude and silence. This yearning for an exclusive contact with the all-consuming Love through monasticism has always been honored by the Church to the same extent as conjugal love. The monks of Upper Egypt, of Mount Sinai, of the deserts of Palestine, and of Mount Athos have established a fifteen-hundred-year tradition of monastic life within the Church. Monasteries are called upon to become true strongholds in the Church's struggle against the internal enemy. It is here that the Church replenishes and nourishes herself with divine energies which then circulate throughout the Body. Thus marriage and the monastic life are two different but complementary ways of communicating with God's love. Both conditions are blessed by the Church. Consequently, priests are chosen from among married men or monastics, and almost never from among celibates living in the world.

CHAPTER 29

SICKNESS AND HEALING
OF THE MEMBERS OF CHRIST'S BODY

A) The Mystery of Repentance

The most serious affliction which can affect a part of the body is to be cut off from the head or the heart. If it no longer receives nervous impulses from the brain, it is paralyzed; if blood from the heart no longer circulates in it, it dies. Similarly, if a member of Christ's Body no longer perceives the will of his Lord, he no longer knows what to do or how to act. Life no longer makes sense to him. And if he no longer receives a current of life and love from the Holy Spirit, he begins to decay and his personality begins to disintegrate. In its most extreme form, this can lead to insanity. Such a break between God and man is called *sin*. Christ, "the Physician of our soul and bodies," is the source of all remedies and cures. When, by the power of the Holy Spirit and the mystery of the Church, Christ's healing hand touches someone who turns to Him begging for the Father's mercy, the sinner is forgiven, healed and reintegrated into the life of the Body. This is called the Mystery of Repentance.

Repentance in the Old Testament
1) The sin of King David (2 Sam 11:2-12:25)

Around 1000 B.C. David, who had previously been anointed by the prophet Samuel, was recognized as king by all the Israelites. He was thirty years old and would reign for forty years (2 Sam 5:4).

He conquered Jerusalem, and it became "the city of David." The Lord was with David and he was victorious in many wars. During a war against the Ammonites, David sent Joab to command the armies, while he himself stayed in Jerusalem. One evening David rose from his couch and strolled on the terrace of the palace, and "he saw from the roof a woman bathing; and the woman was very beautiful" (2 Sam 11:2). He was greatly affected and asked who she was. One of his servants replied, "Is not this Bathsheba, the daughter of Eliam, the wife of Uriah the Hittite?" (v. 3).

David fell in love with Bathsheba, commited adultery with her, and had her husband killed. Then the Lord sent the prophet Nathan to David. He came to the king and said:

> "There were two men in a certain city, the one rich and the other poor. The rich man had very many flocks and herds; but the poor man had nothing but one little ewe lamb, which he had bought. And he brought it up, and it grew up with him and with his children; it used to eat of his morsel, and drink from his cup, and lie in his bosom, and it was like a daughter to him. Now there came a traveler to the rich man, and he was unwilling to take one of his own flock or herd to prepare for the wayfarer who had come to him, but he took the poor man's lamb, and prepared it for the man who had come to him." Then David's anger was greatly kindled against the man; and he said to Nathan, "As the Lord lives, the man who had done this deserves to die; and he shall restore the lamb fourfold, because he did this thing, and because he had no pity."
>
> Nathan said to David, "You are the man . . . Why have you despised the word of the Lord, to do what is evil in His sight? You have smitten Uriah the Hittite with the sword, and have taken his wife to be your wife . . . Now therefore the sword shall never depart from your house." . . . David said to Nathan, "I have sinned against the Lord." (2 Sam 12:2-7, 9-10, 13)

2) David's Repentance

David expressed his repentance in Psalm 50[51] which is now commonly known as the "Miserere" because it begins with the words, "Have mercy upon me," which in Latin is *miserere*. The Church still uses this psalm to express the repentance of sinners and we should recite it whenever we wish to ask God's forgiveness.

Have mercy on me, O God, according to Thy steadfast love;
   according to Thy abundant mercy blot out my transgressions.
Wash me thoroughly from my iniquity,
   and cleanse me from my sin.
For I know my transgressions,
   and my sin is ever before me.
Against Thee, Thee only, have I sinned,
   and done that which is evil in Thy sight,
so that Thou are justified in Thy sentence
   and blameless in Thy judgement.
Behold, I was brought forth in iniquity,
   and in sin did my mother conceive me.
Behold, Thou desirest truth in the inward being;
   therefore teach me wisdom in my secret heart.
Purge me with hyssop, and I shall be clean;
   wash me, and I shall be whiter than snow.
Fill me with joy and gladness;
   let the bones which Thou hast broken rejoice.
Hide Thy face from my sins,
   and blot out all my iniquities.
Create in me a clean heart, O God,
   and put a new and right spirit within me.
Cast me not away from Thy presence,
   and take not Thy holy Spirit from me.
Restore to me the joy of Thy salvation,
   and uphold me with a willing spirit.
Then I will teach transgressors Thy ways,
   and sinners will return to Thee.
Deliver me from blood guiltiness, O God, Thou God of my
salvation,
   and my tongue will sing aloud of Thy deliverance.
O Lord, open Thou my lips,
   and my mouth shall show forth Thy praise.
For Thou hast no delight in sacrifice;
   were I to give a burnt offering, Thou wouldst not be pleased.
The sacrifice acceptable to God is a broken spirit;
   a broken and contrite heart, O God, Thou wilt not despise.
Do good to Zion in Thy good pleasure;
   rebuild the walls of Jerusalem,

> then wilt Thou delight in right sacrifices,
>   in burnt offerings and whole burnt offerings;
> then bulls will be offered on Thy altar.

David's Pardon

Nathan said to David,

> "The Lord also has put away your sin; you shall not die. Neverthe-
> less, because by this deed you have utterly scorned the Lord, the
> child that is born to you shall die." . . . On the seventh day the child
> died . . . Then David comforted his wife, Bathsheba, . . . and she
> bore a son, and he called his name Solomon. And the Lord loved
> him. (2 Sam 12:13-14,18,24)

Repentance in the New Testament

1) The prodigal son (Lk 15:11-32)

A father had two sons. One day the younger one decided to leave
his father's house and asked for his share of the inheritance. The
father gave it to him, and the son went off to a foreign land. Because
of his wealth he was immediately surrounded by false friends who
stayed with him as long as he had money to spend on them. One
day, just as famine began to spread through the land, he realized his
money was gone and so were his friends. To survive, he hired himself
out as a swineherd to a citizen of that country and shared the swine's
food. He fell into the depths of despair. Then he remembered that
he could eat his fill in his father's house, where the servants lived
in far better conditions than his own. So he left everything and
returned to his father's house to ask for employment as a common
laborer. His father saw him in the distance and ran out to meet him.
The son cried out, "Father, I have sinned against heaven and before
you." But before he could finish speaking, the father embraced him
and accepted him as his son. Full of joy, the father ordered his
servants to prepare a banquet and to kill the fatted calf.

The older brother heard the commotion while returning from the
fields and wanted to know what was happening. When he learned
that his wayward brother had returned, he fell into a rage because

he thought that this feasting was unjust. He had always remained faithfully at his father's side and yet had never been given such a feast. But the father said to him, "Son, you are always with me, and all that is mine is yours. It was fitting to make merry and be glad, for this your brother was dead, and is alive; he was lost, and is found."

Seeker: Why is the younger son called "prodigal"?

Sage: "Prodigal" means someone who squanders or wastes his fortune indiscriminately. In other languages he is sometimes called a reveller or debauched. The underlying significance is always the same. He is a juvenile delinquent.[68]

Seeker: What does this parable teach? What does it mean?

Sage: The meaning of this parable can never be exhausted, and this is what it teaches us. You remember how at the beginning of this book we discussed Genesis and the creation and fall of man?[69] Well, the parable of the prodigal son tells the same story, except that Christ concludes His story with a great feast. Remember this parable, for you may find yourself in the same situation someday. The story of the prodigal son is the story of mankind from the very beginning. Human beings are so constituted that we appreciate things only when we lose them. A child who has parents and lives happily does not appreciate this happiness. It is only when he loses everything that he realizes what he has lost. I'm telling you this because I'm also a prodigal son like everyone else. I have not yet returned to my Father, our Father; I have only occasionally had a glimpse of Him, beckoning to me in the distance, because I don't see well.

Seeker: You! A prodigal son! You certainly don't look like one.

Sage: We come into this world and are attracted by it. As we grow up, the distracting perfume of this world turns our heads; we want to see what it's like. And even though we love God, we leave Him to live our own lives, just as sooner or later we leave our earthly

---

68. In his work entitled, *The Pillar and Foundation of the Truth,* the Russian philosopher/scientist/priest Paul Florensky calls the prodigal son "the child who has gone astray": an image of all God's children who fall into sin.

69. Part I, chapter 1, section C.

parents. We go far away and, surrounded by the bustle of the world, gradually forget Him who loves us most and is closest to us. You see what kind of a welcome is promised to us when we return. There is no punishment, for we have already been punished. We have punished ourselves! What a feast, what a response is offered to us by God in response to our own feeble gesture of repentance. As soon as He sees us, He draws us to Himself, even if this displeases the older son.

Seeker: I think the older brother had a point!

Sage: Be careful! The older brother is jealous. And he is hardly disinterested, because he expects to be rewarded for what he thinks are his virtues. Beware of him, for we may be like him, thinking that we have never left the Father's house. The older son had never opened himself to the Father's clemency and generosity, and yet "God is love," and "love bears all things, believes all things, hopes all things, endures all things" (1 Cor 13:7).

The healing of the paralytic at Capernaum (Mt 9:1-8; Mk 2:1-12; Lk 5:17-26)

One day Jesus was in a house preaching to a multitude of people. Among them were Pharisees (members of a Jewish sect who strictly observed the Mosaic Law) and scribes (doctors of the Law). They were learned, sometimes proud and hypocritical men, more anxious to defend the letter of the Law than to accept the Good News of God's Kingdom and its grace.

As usually happened whenever Jesus preached, great crowds gathered to listen and to be healed, so that there was no room even to squeeze through the door.

Four men came carrying a paralytic on a litter. They tried to enter so that they could put the man in front of Jesus, but were unable to get through. This, however, did not discourage them. They climbed up on the flat roof of the house, removed some tiles (or thatch) and lowered the pallet through this hole. (We must remember that houses in that region were contructed of light materials and were not firmly nailed together.)

"And when He saw their faith He said, 'Man, your sins are forgiven you'" (Lk 5:20). Notice that Jesus did not say, "Be healed," but rather, "Your sins are forgiven you." For Jesus heals the whole man. He has the power both to forgive and also to heal all afflictions, and we should never separate these two.

Jesus knew that the scribes and Pharisees were asking themselves, "Who is this that speaks blasphemies? Who can forgive sins but God only?"; so He said:

> "Why do you question in your hearts? Which is easier, to say, 'Your sins are forgiven you,' or to say, 'Rise and walk'? But that you may know that the Son of man has authority on earth to forgive sins"— He said to the man who was paralyzed—"I say to you rise, and take up your bed and go home." And immediately he rose before them, and took up that on which he lay, and went home, glorifying God. (Lk 5:22-25)

There is another very important aspect to this narrative besides the healing itself and Christ's lesson to the Pharisees. And that is the attitude of the men who took so much trouble and so ingeniously lowered the invalid's bed through the roof to Jesus' feet. In fact we read that it is upon seeing their faith that Jesus pardons and heals their friend.

We should be well aware that when we pray, asking the Lord for something either for ourselves or for others, we also are asked to participate actively. Above all we must have faith and courage, but we must also struggle against laziness and selfishness. The paralytic's friends expended a lot of effort, intelligence and faith to help the invalid. They showed their confidence in God, as well as their love for God and their neighbor. This is asked of us also. The newly healed paralytic and his friends probably returned home profoundly changed. They became new men, conscious that they were forgiven, healed and loved. They understood that one of man's fundamental needs is the forgiveness of his sins; that forgiveness is even more important than the healing of physical ailments because it is through repentance that God grants healing.

"That you may know that the Son of man has authority on earth to forgive sins . . . I say to you, Rise, take up your bed and go home."

This is the key sentence of this Gospel narrative. By healing the paralytic of a visible ailment, the paralysis of his body, Jesus showed us that He had already freed him from sin, a far more serious affliction. God made man, the Son of God who became the Son of man, forgives sins. He will pay for this power with His own most precious Blood when He dies upon the Cross. He will obtain divine forgiveness for others by submitting to punishment by sinners, for death is the natural consequence of sin. How can a branch which has been cut off from the tree survive? "Father, forgive them, for they know not what they do." He heals us by bringing us back to God. But let us discuss how Christ can grant us forgiveness today, in practical and concrete terms.

The Mystery of the Sacrament of Repentance

As we have already seen, the Lord Jesus acts in the world today through the Holy Spirit, who transforms the Church into His Body. The forgiving and healing hand of the Lord Jesus reaches us through the Church and the Holy Spirit. As Jesus said to His apostles on the day of the Resurrection, "Receive the Holy Spirit. If you forgive the sins of any, they are forgiven; if you retain the sins of any, they are retained" (Jn 20:22-23).

But we must sincerely desire forgiveness and be eager to ask for it. The parable of the prodigal son, which we have just discussed, illustrates the stages through which we must pass on our return from death to life.

1. The prodigal son "came to himself," became aware of his degradation and decided to return to his father's house. This is conversion or *metanoia*.

2. He admits his sin and says, "Father, I have sinned against heaven and before you." This is confession.

3. The Father, who never stopped waiting for him runs out as soon as he sees him and embraces him before he finishes confessing. This is forgiveness.

4. The fatted calf is killed. This is the feast, the eucharistic banquet.

We also must go through the same four stages.

1. *Metanoia*

At this point one's conscience becomes enlightened. It is at this moment that David understood Nathan's words, "It is you," after hearing the story of the poor man from whom the rich man had stolen a lamb. The Greek word *metanoia* means "turning of the Spirit"; it signifies an inward change, a conversion. It is the discovery that one is sick, accompanied by the desire to be healed; the most serious illness is the one which is ignored. Finally, it is an awakening: "Awake, O sleeper, and arise from the dead, and Christ shall give you light" (Eph 5:14).

Sin is a state of lethargy, a deathly condition. Repentance is the thirst for life, for the true life, the full life which is found only in God. It is man's answer to the words of God Himself, as reported by the prophet Ezekiel, "I have no pleasure in the death of the wicked, but that the wicked turn from his way and live" (Ezek 33:11).

2. *Confession*

When we do evil, the whole Body of Christ suffers, for "if one member suffers, all suffer together" (1 Cor 12:26). When we sin, we harm not only ourselves but the whole Church. That is why the apostle James says, "Therefore confess your sins to one another, and pray for one another, that you may be healed" (Jas 5:16).

Three kinds of sins in particular estrange us from God and have always resulted in the temporary exclusion of the faithful from the Church.

a) Apostasy, the sin against God

Apostasy is the denial of Christ. We refuse to admit that we are His disciples either from shame or fear: "whoever denies Me before men, I also will deny before My Father who is in heaven" (Mt 10:33). This was the sin of those who during times of persecution said that they were no longer Christians. Today it is the sin of those who, for fear of "making a bad impression," allow themselves to be lured into following fashionable trends, to act like unbelievers.

b) Murder, the sin against one's neighbor

This includes not only the one who kills, but also the one who hates; for "anyone who hates his brother is a murderer," as the apostle John tells us (1 Jn 3:15). To hate is to kill in spirit. Anyone who refuses to forgive and holds a grudge commits the same sin. "If you do not forgive men their trespasses, neither will your Father forgive your trespasses" (Mt 6:15). See also the parable of the debtors (Mt 18:23-35). "If you do not forgive your brother from your heart," the heavenly Father will treat you the same way He did the unkind debtor. That is why St. Paul tells us, "Be angry but do not sin; do not let the sun go down on your anger" (Eph 4:26).

c) Concupiscence, the sin against love and oneself

This sin is the pursuit of carnal pleasure without love, without a total giving of oneself to the other. It is the sin *against* the flesh and not, as it is often incorrectly defined, *of* the flesh. It is the sin of one who "sins against his own body" (1 Cor 6:18), who sins against love, who profanes love. And we communicate with God through love, for He is love (1 Jn 4:16). Therefore, anyone who profanes love rejects God, "for God has not called us for uncleanness, but in holiness. Therefore whoever disregards this, disregards not man but God, who gives His Holy Spirit to you" (1 Thess 4:7-8).

> Do you not know that your bodies are members of Christ? Shall I therefore take the members of Christ and make them members of a prostitute? Never! Do you not know that he who joins himself to a prostitute becomes one body with her? For, as it is written, "The two shall become one flesh." . . . Do you not know that your body is a temple of the Holy Spirit within you, which you have from God? You are not your own, you were bought with a price. So glorify God in your body. (1 Cor 6:15-16, 19-20)

Anyone who commits these sins must repent and ask to be accepted once more as a member of Christ's Body. This Body, the Church, must agree to accept him back; the congregation must forgive him. The sinner must come to Church, acknowledge his sin, and confess it to the congregation. That is why confession was public in the early Church. However, this presented serious problems because some members of the congregation remembered the sins which had been confessed and continued to distrust the sinner even after he had received forgiveness. Therefore, it gradually became customary for the head of the congregation, the bishop or priest, to hear the penitent's confession privately.

Confession expresses the sincerity of one's repentance. It is the return of the prodigal to his Father's house. The priest who listens to the penitent represents the Church, the whole suffering Body of Christ, consisting of the congregation and its head, Christ. He himself is only a humble witness.

3. Pardon or Absolution

In order for the congregation to readmit its wayward but repentant member and to reconcile him to the other members and their common Lord, it must grant him forgiveness from Him who has power to forgive sins, the Head of the Body, Christ Himself. And so the priest puts his hand on the stole which he had draped over the penitent's head and says in the name of Christ and the congregation: "All that you have confessed to my humble person . . . may God forgive it you both in this world and in the world to come. May our Lord and God and Savior Jesus Christ, through His grace and love for mankind, forgive you, my child, all your sins and trangressions . . ." (Greek usage; other traditions use somewhat different formulas.)

This is the absolution. The Holy Spirit grants Christ's pardon and healing to the penitent. Through the mystery of the Church and by means of the forgiveness expressed by the congregation and its priest. The penitent is now "whiter than snow." St Isaac the Syrian, a monk of the seventh century, tells us: "In comparison with God's mercy, the sins of mankind are but a handful of sand in the sea." Silouan, another great monk who died in 1938, said: "A man who is no longer at peace with himself should repent and the Lord will forgive his sins. Then joy and peace will reign again in his soul."

For he is now reconciled with God and man. Forgiveness means the reconciliation of man and his Lord, the reestablishment of the natural link which allows the creature to communicate with the Creator.

> All this is from God, who through Christ reconciled us to Himself and gave us the ministry of reconciliation; that is, in Christ God was reconciling the world to Himself, not counting their trespasses against them, and entrusting to us the message of reconciliation. (2 Cor 5:18-19)

> But God shows His love for us in that while we were yet sinners Christ died for us. . . . For if while we were enemies we were reconciled to God by the death of His Son, much more, now that we are reconciled, shall we be saved by His life. (Rom 5:8,10)

God's forgiveness through Jesus Christ gives us back true life and delivers us from death. Let us listen to St Paul again: "We beseech you on behalf of Christ, be reconciled to God" (2 Cor 5:20), so that we can exclaim with him, "we also rejoice in God through our Lord Jesus Christ, through whom we have now received our reconciliation" (Rom 5:11). The sinner who is forgiven becomes once again a part of Christ's Body.

4. The Celebration

The sinner can now approach the Holy Mysteries as freely as he had formerly done, to communicate of the Body and Blood of Christ the Savior, to drink at the well of Eternal Life, and to receive immortality. The Mystery of Repentance is followed by the Mystery of the Eucharist; the sinner is healed and saved.

B) The Mystery of Holy Unction

Man is a whole, composed of both body and soul. As St Gregory Palamas said in the fourteenth century, "The name 'man' is given to body and soul together, for man in his totality was created in the image of God." St Irenaeus also tells us that Christ is the Savior of both body and soul; if He did not save our body, He could not save us at all, for who has ever seen a man without a body?

That is why Christ healed infirmities of the body as well as of the spirit. The Gospels are full of stories about seriously ill people who were healed by Jesus: paralytics, blind, deaf and dumb, lepers, epileptics, and those possessed by the devil. The apostles continued this work, "they cast out many demons, and anointed with oil many that were sick and healed them" (Mk 6:13). This work of healing continues in the Church today, through the Holy Spirit and the mystery of the anointing of the sick.

The sacrament of anointing, or Holy Unction, is meant for any sick person, regardless of the seriousness of his condition, and is always administered in the hope of his recovery. It is, therefore, wrong to call this "extreme unction," as if the sacrament could only be administered once, without any hope of recovery, in the last moments of life.

We can clearly see how wrong this position is by reading Jas 5:14-15:

> Is any one among you sick? Let him call for the elders of the Church, and let them pray over him, anointing him with oil in the name of the Lord; and the prayer of faith will save the sick man, and the Lord will raise him up; and if he has committed sins, he will be forgiven.

It is clear from these words of the apostle that there are no precise boundaries between sickness of the body and sickness of the soul; even medical science is well aware of this. That is why throughout the sacrament of Unction, we pray both for the healing of the body and for the pardon of the sick person's sins. We ask for his healing in the context of repentance and salvation, and not as an end in itself. Life—true, eternal life—does not end with man's death. No matter what the outcome of the sickness is, whether the person recovers or dies, he needs to repent and to receive divine forgiveness. This is true healing. Through Holy Unction and its powerful prayer, the Church reminds the one who is sick that he is not alone, that the Church is present at this side. When one of its members suffers, the whole congregation suffers (1 Cor 12:26). Therefore, the whole congregation asks for forgiveness, help, and deliverance from the vicious cycle of sin and suffering, through the prayer of its priests. The grace of God heals the infirmities of body and soul.

Thus the sacrament of Unction can bring healing to the invalid, or in any case give the strength and hope he needs. The Church does not take the place of the doctor after he has exhausted all the resources of medical science. Rather, it tries to being the anguished sufferer into contact with God's love and life. In Christ joy and suffering, health and sickness, life and death, can all lead to Life. We are called upon to make our way to God with confidence either here on earth, if we recover, or in heaven if we do not. We must continue to sing God's glory and say, "Have mercy upon me, a sinner," in a spirit of submission to God's will. We must also be full of confidence and humility, putting our trust in divine mercy.

The sacrament of Holy Unction can be performed either in church in the presence of the congregation, if the sick person can be brought there, or at home if he cannot be moved. Seven priests should officiate at this service, although it can also be performed by three, two, or even one. On Wednesday of Holy Week, in many parishes the sacrament of Holy Unction is administered to all the faithful for the healing of their infirmities and "forgotten sins." The service consists of:

1. Seven prayers for blessing the oil, called in Greek *euchelaion*. Then, following the teaching of the apostles, the priests anoint the forehead, nostrils, temples, mouth, chest, back, and hands of the sick person with the "oil of mercy." One of the prayers begins: "Holy Father, Physician of our souls and bodies, Thou hast sent Thine only Son, our Lord Jesus Christ, to heal all sickness and to deliver us from death: heal the spiritual and bodily weakness of Thy servant."

2. The reading of seven passages from the Epistles and Gospels. These passages show the Lord Jesus' love for the sick and for sinners. It is a hymn praising God's love and mercy. We should also note that *eleos* means mercy or compassion in Greek, and *elaion* means oil, so that oil very naturally became the symbol of divine mercy. In the parable of the good Samaritan we read, "But a

Samaritan . . . came to where he was; and when he saw him, he had compassion [*eleos*], and went to him and bound up his wounds, pouring on oil [*elaion*] and wine" (Lk 10:33-34). Similarly, in the parable of the ten virgins, the oil with which the five wise virgins dress their lamps represents the mercy with which every Christian should fortify himself.

The seven Epistles, seven Gospels, seven priests, and seven anointings by the seven priests, indicate to us that the sacrament of Holy Unction involves the whole Church, the entire Body of Christ. It is not simply the individual prayer of a particular healer.

CHAPTER 30

CONCLUSION

Since the thirteenth century, it has been the custom of the Church to speak of "seven sacraments" (*mysteria* or Mysteries): Baptism, Chrismation (Confirmation), Eucharist, Repentance (Confession), Ordination, Marriage, and Anointing of the Sick. In exploring the meaning of these sacraments, we have discovered that they actually represent various aspects of one single Mystery, i.e. the Mystery of Christ, which is also the Mystery of His Resurrected Body, the Mystery of His Church, and the Mystery of God's presence in the midst of the faithful and of the whole world. We live this Mystery by taking part in the divine Eucharist. Through the Eucharist we are able to participate in the Mystery of Christ and the Church. We have seen that we enter the eucharistic assembly and become members of Christ's Body through the Mysteries of Baptism and Chrismation. The Mystery of Repentance allows us to return to the Church after we have excluded ourselves through sin. New families are integrated into the body of the Church through the Mystery of Marriage (crowning). The Mystery of Unction with holy oil enables infirm members once again to participate fully in the life of the Body. And finally, the eucharistic assembly, the Body of Christ, is given structure and organization through the Mystery of Ordination. In short, all the sacraments contribute to the fullness of the eucharistic mystery and flow into it; they are manifestations of the unique Mystery of Christ who lives in the Church through His Holy Spirit.

The sacraments are not simply human acts; they are in essence manifestations of Pentecost, the work of the Holy Spirit. They confirm Christ's Word,[70] allowing us to take part in the unfathomable

---

70. The origin of all the sacraments can be traced to words spoken by Christ or the apostles. This serves as a guarantee, an objective criterion, for the work of the

riches which are hidden in them. They unite us mysteriously to the Body of the Risen One and the work which He has accomplished for the world.

Being so greatly honored by our Savior, we should exclaim with St Paul,

> I am sure that neither death, nor life, nor angels, nor principalities, nor things present, nor things to come, nor powers, nor height, nor depth, nor anything else in all creation, will be able to separate us from the love of God in Jesus Christ our Lord. (Rom 8:38-39)

Holy Spirit who comes to confirm the Son's word. "Go . . . baptizing them in the name of the Father and of the Son and of the Holy Spirit" (Mt 28:19; Baptism); "The Spirit was given through the laying on of the apostles' hands" (Acts 8:19; Chrismation); "Take, eat, this is My body" (Mt 26:26; Eucharist); "If you forgive the sins of any, they are forgiven" (Jn 20:22; Confession); "The husband is the head of the wife as Christ is the head of the church" (Eph 5:22; Marriage); "Is any among you sick? Let him call for the elders of the church" (Jas 5:14; Unction); "Do not neglect the gift you have, which was given you by prophetic utterance when the council of elders laid their hands upon you" (1 Tim 4:14; Ordination). These words are necessary if we are to call an act of the Church "God's mystery" and see it as the revelation of the great Mystery of Christ.

Part VII

The Second Coming and The Life of The World to Come

Introduction

In the Creed we proclaim, "He shall come again with glory to judge the living and the dead, whose kingdom shall have no end." The Second Coming of the Lord Jesus, His return in glory at the end of time and the establishment of His Kingdom, is the central theme of the seventh and last part of our book.

When we consider the end of time, our own destiny is of paramount importance to us. The problem of what will happen to "me" is fundamental to the basic question, "What will happen to me when I die?" Every one of us thinks of himself as the center of the universe, but in biblical revelation and in the Tradition of the Church (Apostolic Tradition[1]), the center of the universe is not "I" but He who said: "I am the Alpha and Omega, the beginning and the end." The question which the Bible answers is, "What will happen when Christ returns?"

The Church lives in anticipation of the Lord's return, of the end of time, the "day of Lord," the "second and glorious Coming." These

---

1. Apostolic Tradition or Holy Tradition is the Word of God which enters into the hearts of the apostles through the Holy Spirit, and which this same Spirit transmits to the conscience of theChurch. This Word is thus lived within the Church and is expressed by a manner of life, by gestures, writings, ways of thinking, praying, and acting which characterize the Body of Christ, of Christ who is the same both when he speaks through Scripture and when he lives in his Church.

terms describe a completely new world which the Old Testament prophets and the authors of the New Testament describe to us. They often use symbolic language to express what human language cannot express, using an interplay of themes, traditions and revelations. The result is an awe-inspiring global vision which is difficult to interpret, like the design of a tapestry composed of many intertwined threads. But like the pilgrims of Emmaus, Christians read the Scriptures enlightened by the light of knowledge which comes from meeting the Lord Jesus. Then all these themes fall into place around His Second Coming.

CHAPTER 31

THE FIRST AND SECOND COMINGS
OF THE LORD

A) In the Old Testament

In reading certain passages of the Old Testament, and in particular the Book of Isaiah, one might get the impression that the Messiah will come only once in order to establish an era of reconciliation, justice, glory, and happiness. "There shall come forth a shoot from the stump of Jesse [the father of David] . . . with righteousness he shall judge the poor . . . and with the breath of his lips he shall slay the wicked . . . The wolf shall dwell with the lamb . . . The sucking child shall play over the hole of the asp . . . They shall not hurt or destroy in all my holy mountain; for the earth shall be full of the knowledge of the Lord" (Is 11:1, 4, 6, 8-9). And again, "On this mountain the Lord of hosts will make for all peoples a feast . . . He will swallow up death for ever, and the Lord God will wipe away tears from all faces, and the reproach of His people He will take away from all the earth . . . It will be said on that day, 'Lo, this is our God; we have waited for Him, that He might save us . . . Let us be glad and rejoice in His salvation'" (Is 25:6, 8-9).

Seeker: The Messiah did come more than two thousand years ago, but instead of seeing the wolf playing with the lamb and death disappearing, I see the cruel and powerful oppressing and exploiting the weak, violence unleashed everywhere, and the dead filling up the cemeteries.

Sage: Alas, that's true! But wait a minute. You know that in this book we always read the Old Testament in the light of what Christ has revealed to us. If we read the Book of Isaiah and similar passages in Daniel, Zechariah and Malachi, we see that there is a telescoping of two planes in this global vision of the messianic era. When we look from a distance at two mountains which are actually very far apart, they both appear on the same plane, but as we come near the closer one, it becomes apparent that the second one is much farther away. Similarly, in the prophets we can distinguish two points of view about the coming of the Messiah which seem at first glance contradictory. But this contradiction disappears if we accept the idea that they relate to two successive comings of the same Messiah.

In reading the Old Testament texts we are no longer covered with the veil which darkened the hearts of those who had not yet seen Jesus the Messiah. This veil disappears in Christ; it is removed through our conversion (2 Cor 3:14-16).

The Book of Isaiah

On one hand the Book of Isaiah describes the Messiah as a suffering servant who is beaten and humiliated.

> . . . his appearance was so marred, beyond human semblance, . . . he was wounded for our transgressions, he was bruised for our iniquities; . . . The righteous one, my servant, shall make many to be accounted rightous; and he shall bear their iniquities . . . He poured out his soul to death, and was numbered with the transgressors; yet he bore the sin of many, and made intercession for the transgressors (Is 52:14, 53:5, 11, 12).

On the other hand, the same book describes the Messiah as coming in glory, even in God's own glory. Jesus Himself alludes to this passage (Is 35:1-10), when the disciples of the imprisoned John the Baptist ask Him if He is "the One who is to come" (Mt 11:2-6). This text is read on Theophany at the blessing of the water:

> The wilderness and the dry land shall be glad, the desert shall rejoice and blossom . . . and rejoice with joy and singing. The glory of Lebanon shall be given to it, the majesty of Carmel and Sharon. They shall see the glory of the Lord, the majesty of our God . . . Say to those who are of a fearful heart, "Be strong, fear not! Behold, your God . . . will come to save you." Then the eyes of the blind

shall be opened, and the ears of the deaf unstopped; then shall the lame man leap like a hart[2] . . . For waters shall break forth in the wilderness, and streams in the desert . . . (Is 35:1-2, 4-6)

Seeker: These two passages present totally contradictory images of the Messiah.

Sage: They are not contradictory if we apply the first of these texts to the first coming of the Messiah, in which He announces the Kingdom of God to a hostile world: "He was in the world . . . yet the world knew Him not. He came to His own home, and His own people received Him not. . . . The light shines in the darkness, and the darkness has not overcome it" (Jn 1:5-11). The second text refers to the Second Coming which the Lord Jesus Himself foretells when He promises to return in glory. The messianic era initiated by the Incarnation can only be established with the collaboration of mankind. This collaboration is called synergy. We prepare for the Second Coming, the final triumph of justice and life over evil and death, by becoming united by faith to the crucified and risen Savior. Then the wolf and the lamb will be truly reconciled.

The Book of Daniel

This book describes two visions of the first and second Comings of the Messiah.

1) The first vision

The first vision consists of King Nebuchadnezzar's[3] allegorical dream which the prophet interprets. The central image in this dream is a rock that grows and expands.

The king sees a statue of great size, with a bright and terrifying aspect. Its head is of fine gold, its breast and arms are of silver, its

---

2. The miraculous healings performed by the Lord Jesus during his first coming are also signs foreshadowing the glory he will reveal when he returns at the end of time.

3. Nebuchadnezzar was King of Babylon from 604 to 562 B.C. In 587, he conquered Jerusalem and sent the Israelites into exile in Babylon. There they remained until 538, when the Persian conqueror Cyrus allowed them to return to Jerusalem.

stomach and thighs are of bronze, its legs are of iron, and its feet are partly of iron and partly of clay. Suddenly a rock crashed down on the feet of the statue and smashed it. The clay, iron, bronze, silver, and gold were all broken in pieces and scattered, without leaving a trace. And the rock grew into a great mountain that filled the whole earth (Dan 2:31-35).

Daniel interprets the four elements of which the statue is made as a succession of four great kingdoms. The last kingdom, symbolized by the feet, is a divided kingdom which is both strong and weak. The rock is also a kingdom, but unlike the others, it is established by the God of heaven. Daniel explains: "The God of heaven will set up a kingdom which shall never be destroyed, nor shall its sovereignty be left to another people. It shall break in pieces all these kingdoms and bring them to an end, and it shall stand forever" (Dan 2:44).

This rock, which is cut out without the help of human hands and smashes the great statue, gradually fills up the whole world. It overthrows all earthly kingdoms (note the disturbing—even subversive—element in the Kingdom of God, which permits it to attack the kingdoms of this world), and symbolizes the historical events initiated by the appearance of the Messiah. This passage is read on Christmas Eve because the Church interprets it as a prediction of the Messiah's first coming, inaugurating His kingdom in this world.

> Christ, the cornerstone not cut by the hand of man, was taken from you, the unhewn mountain, O Virgin; joining in one two different natures. Therefore we magnify you, O Theotokos, with great rejoicing. (Irmos, ninth ode, tone 4 Sunday matins canon)

In this hymn Daniel's mountain is interpreted as a prefiguration of the Theotokos. The Rock is the image of Christ, born of the Virgin without the intervention of an earthly father. This Rock is also the cornerstone of Psalm 117 [118]:22, which is rejected by the builders but in fact supports the whole building. It is also the precious cornerstone revealed to Isaiah, which St Peter in his First Epistle recognizes as Christ, the "living stone" (Is 28:16; 1 Pet 2:4).

2) *The second vision*

In chapter 7 of the Book of Daniel, the prophet cries out:

> I saw in the night visions, and behold, with the clouds of heaven there came one like a son of man, and he came to the Ancient of Days and was presented before him. And to him was given dominion and glory and kingship, that all peoples, nations, and languages should serve him; his dominion is an everlasting dominion, which shall not pass away,[4] and his kingdom one that shall not be destroyed. (Dan 7:13-14)

Clearly this passage refers to the same kingdom. The king appears "with the clouds of heaven" and stands before the throne of the heavenly Father, the Ancient of Days. Christ applies this prophecy to Himself when He foretells His return in glory (Mt 24:30). He also quotes the passage to Caiaphas, thus provoking the high priest to condemn Him to death as a blasphemer (Mt 26:64).

The Prophet Zechariah

Zechariah also describes the Messiah both as humble and suffering, and as all-powerful and glorious.

a) The Humble and Suffering Messiah

"Lo, your king comes to you . . . humble and riding on an ass, on a colt the foal of an ass" (Zech 9:9). The evangelist John (12:16) tells us that after the Resurrection Jesus' disciples "remembered that this had been written of Him and had been done to Him" on Palm Sunday at His entrance into Jerusalem. The prophet Zechariah writes in chapter 12:10, 12:

> . . . when they look on him whom they have pierced, they shall mourn for him, as one mourns for an only child, and weep bitterly over him, as one weeps over a first-born. . . .
> The land shall mourn.

---

4. This verse is cited by the Archangel Gabriel during the Annunciation to the Virgin Mary, and again in the Symbol of Faith or Creed: "His Kingdom shall have no end."

b) The Glorious and All-powerful Christ

But in chapter 14:4-5, 7, 9, Zechariah describes a glorious and all-powerful Christ:

> On that day his feet shall stand on the Mount of Olives which lies
> before Jerusalem on the east; and the Mount of Olives shall be split
> in two . . . Then the Lord your God will come, and all the holy
> ones with him . . . And there shall be continuous day . . . And the
> Lord will become king over all the earth; on that day the Lord will
> be one and His name one.

B) *In the New Testament*

The Messiah prophesied His Second Coming during His earthly ministry: ". . . and they will see the Son of man coming on the clouds of heaven with power and great glory; and He will send out His angels with a loud trumpet call, and they will gather His elect from the four winds, from one end of heaven to the other" (Mt 24:30-31; Mk 13:26-27; Lk 21:27).

In his very first letter written to the Thessalonians around 50 A.D., St. Paul reminds us of this promise of the Lord Jesus: "This we declare to you by the word of the Lord . . . The Lord Himself will descend from heaven with a cry of command, with the archangel's call, and with the sound of the trumpet of God" (1 Thess 4:15-16). "For as the lightning comes from the east and shines as far as the west, so will be the coming of the Son of Man" (Mt 24:27).

As for the time, neither we nor the angels in heaven, nor even the Son of Man, know the day or the hour, but only the Father (Mt 24:36). That is why Jesus tells us to watch, for "the day of the Lord will come like a thief," "therefore you also must be ready" (2 Pet 3:10; Mt 24:44).

CHAPTER 32

EXPECTATION OF THE SECOND COMING: VIGILANCE

Jesus tells us that the believer must always be vigilant. To be vigilant is to be ready: ready for the Kingdom, ready to greet the Lord. In the parable of the ten virgins which we discussed in relation to the Church as the bride of Christ,[5] the wise virgins watch, making sure that they have oil in their lamps, i.e., the action of the Holy Spirit in their hearts. Jesus also gave us the parable of the faithful servant whom the master finds watching when he returns unexpectedly. The Church has incorporated the theme of these parables in the solemn matins of Holy Monday, Tuesday and Wednesday. Every believer seeks through these hymns to identify with the wise virgins and the watchful servant.

The state of spiritual watchfulness is not simply the opposite of physiological sleep. The watchfulness which Jesus expects of us is like the watchfulness of a sentinel, alert to the slightest sign of the presence of the enemy. It is a state of constant spiritual struggle, the opposite of spiritual sleep in which man allows himself to be controlled by events, like an automaton in a life which passes like a dream. If we are in such a state of withdrawn somnabulance, the Kingdom cannot grow within us. Thus, addressing the Ephesians, St Paul says, "Awake, O sleeper, and arise from the dead, and Christ shall give you light" (Eph 5:14).

He also writes, "Pray without ceasing" (1 Thess 5:17). This is one way in which we can obey the Lord's injunction to watch. Orthodox spiritual tradition links vigilance with perpetual prayer. This tradition is illustrated in *The Way of the Pilgrim*. In this book a simple

5. See page 266.

peasant asks the question, what is meant by "Pray without ceasing"? He becomes a pilgrim and eventually finds an answer in the teaching of perpetual prayer. This prayer flows not from the lips but from the heart, allowing one to repeat the name of Jesus without ceasing. It is the "prayer of the heart," or the "Jesus prayer," in which we repeat constantly: "Lord Jesus Christ, Son of God, have mercy on me, a sinner."

The members of the Church live together in love, forgiveness, reconciliation, and humility. They act as "sons of light" (Jn 12:36). They show the world that night is past and that the Day of the Lord is close at hand (Rom 13:12). They anticipate and hasten the coming of this day by being vigilant (2 Pet 3:12).

CHAPTER 33

SIGNS FORETELLING THE SECOND COMING

When the Lord urged the disciples to be prepared for His return, they asked Him to be more specific. "Tell us, when will this be, and what will be the sign when these things are all to be accomplished?" (Mk 13:4, Mt 24:4; Lk 21:7). The Lord Jesus refused to give them a precise date but revealed certain signs which will confirm His word and remind us of the imminent coming of the Bridegroom. The Bridegroom delays His coming, but He will nevertheless appear when we least expect Him. Let us discuss these signs in the order in which they appear in the Gospel according to St Matthew. Some of them are historical events and some are present in the world today, so that it is impossible to speak of them in chronological order.

A) "There will not be left here one stone upon another . . ." (Mt 24:2)

The Lord Jesus first speaks of His Second Coming as He and His disciples stand in awe before the splendor of the Temple in Jerusalem, newly rebuilt by King Herod[6] (Mk 13:1). He tells the disciples that the destruction of the Temple will be the first sign of the coming end: "You see all these, do you not? Truly, I say to you, there will not be left here one stone upon another that will not be thrown down" (Mt 24:2). Furthermore:

"When you see Jerusalem surrounded by armies, then know that its desolation has come near. Then let those who are in Judea flee to the mountains, and let those who are inside the city depart, and let not those who are out in the country enter it; for these are the days of vengeance, to fulfill all that is written. Alas for those who

6. The project was begun c. 19 B.C., and took forty-six years to complete. Cf Jn 2:20.

are with child and for those who give suck in those days! For great distress shall be upon the earth and wrath upon this people. They will fall by the edge of the sword and be led captive among all nations; and Jerusalem will be trodden down by the Gentiles, until the times of the Gentiles are fulfilled." (Lk 21:20-24)

This prophecy was fulfilled forty years later in 70 A.D. when Titus besieged Jerusalem, razed the city, and burned the Temple. The inhabitants were killed, sold into slavery, or condemned to forced labor. Remembering the words of their Lord, the disciples saw these events as the fulfillment of His prophecy. The destruction of Jerusalem remains the symbol of the end of the world. This is one of the reasons why events in the Holy Land are of concern to us (see Ps 86[87]:5).

B) "Many will come in My name, saying, 'I am the Christ'" (Mt 24:5)

"Take heed that no one leads you astray. For many will come in My name, saying, 'I am the Christ,' and they will lead many astray" (Mt 24:4-5; Mk 13:6; Lk 21:8).

History has already produced many false Christs and will produce others in the future. Only by living in the Church can we avoid being seduced by them.

C) "And you will hear of wars and rumors of wars . . ." (Mt 24:6)

"And you will hear of wars and rumors of wars. See that you are not alarmed; for this must take place, but the end is not yet. For nation will rise against nation, and kingdom against kingdom, and there will be famines and earthquakes in various places. All this is but the beginning of the birth-pangs." (Mt 24:6-8; Mk 13:7-8; Lk 21:9-11)

D) "Then they will deliver you up to tribulation, and put you to death . . ." (Mt 24:9)

"Then they will deliver you up to tribulation and put you to death; and you will be hated by all nations for My name's sake. And then many will fall away and betray one another, and hate one another." (Mt 24:9-10)

"But take heed to yourselves. For they will deliver you up to councils, and you will be beaten in synagogues, and you will stand before governors and kings for My sake, to bear testimony before them." (Mk 13:9)

"Settle it therefore in your minds, not to meditate beforehand how to answer. For I will give you a mouth and wisdom, which none of your adversaries will be able to withstand or contradict. You will be delivered up even by parents and brothers and kinsmen and friends, and some of you they will put to death. You will be hated by all for My name's sake. But not a hair of your head will perish. By your endurance you will gain your lives." (Lk 21:14-19)

These words are echoed by the Beatitudes, "Blessed are you when men revile you and persecute you . . . on my account." This encouraged the martyrs of the first three centuries of our era to resist their persecutors and to make the Church fertile with their precious blood so that the whole Roman Empire was converted. Later there were persecutions in missionary countries. In our own day persecutions have occurred with a renewed intensity in many countries which had long been Christian. Furthermore, the Church must now prepare herself to confront contemporary neo-paganism, a frigid monster, frightening in the efficiency of the technology and science which it places at the disposal of power and pleasure seeking.

E) ". . . wickedness is multiplied . . ." (Mt 24:12)

It is naively optimistic to think that mankind improves with every generation, as if moral progress went hand in hand with scientific progress.

On the contrary, the Lord warns us that before His return, "because wickedness is multiplied,[7] most men's love will grow cold" (Mt 24:12).

---

7. Wickedness or iniquity is conduct in opposition to the Law of God, which is equity and justice.

"For then there will be great tribulation, such as has not been from the beginning of the world until now, no, and never will be. And if those days had not been shortened, no human being would be saved; but for the sake of the elect those days will be shortened." (Mt 24:21-22)

The Lord Himself asks, ". . . when the Son of man comes, will He find faith on earth?" (Lk 18:8)

St Paul also speaks of coming tribulations in his letter to Timothy:

But understand this, that in the last days there will come times of distress. For men will be lovers of self, lovers of money, proud, arrogant, abusive, disobedient to their parents, ungrateful, unholy, inhuman, implacable, slanderers, profligates, fierce, haters of good, treacherous, reckless, swollen with conceit, lovers of pleasure rather then lovers of God, holding the form of religion but denying the power of it. Avoid such people. (2 Tim 3:1-5)

Today we are witnessing an outburst of pride and unbelief, together with an upsurge of delinquency and criminality. Large-scale crimes are committed by states, and the monstrous and satanic use of torture by governments of the most diverse political persuasions is widespread. Let us not be intimidated or discouraged by this, but rather let us resist with courage and tenacity. The Lord Jesus has given us strength to confront these trials by foretelling them, so that they are signs of His imminent return. The more clearly the Evil One manifests himself, the more faithful we should be, for "he who endures to the end will be saved" (Mt 24:13).

F) "And this gospel of the kingdom will be preached throughout the whole world . . ." (Mt 24:14)

"And this gospel of the kingdom will be preached throughout the whole world, as a testimony to all nations; and then the end will come" (Mt 24:14).

The Lord brings the Good News, not only so that it may bear fruit in the hearts of those who have heard it, but also so that it may be announced to all nations before His return. That is why Jesus sent the disciples two by two into all the cities and places where He Himself would go. He told them:

> "The harvest is plentiful, but the laborers are few. Pray therefore the Lord of the harvest to send out laborers into his harvest. Go your way; behold, I send you out as lambs in the midst of wolves. Carry no purse, no bag, no sandals . . . Whatever house you enter, first say, 'Peace be to this house!' And if a son of peace is there, your peace shall rest upon him; but if not, it shall return to you . . . Whenever you enter a town and they receive you, eat what is set before you. Heal the sick in it and say to them: 'The kingdom of God has come near to you.'" (Lk 10:2-6, 8-9)

At this time Jesus was preaching to the Jews, for the Kingdom must first announced to Israel. To accomplish this mission, Jesus sent His disciples ahead into Judea and Galilee. He sent them empty-handed, like innocent and godly children, with only the fruitful word to sow for future harvests.

But when His mission was accomplished and the Cross was about to be erected, just before His last vigil on the Mount of Olives, Jesus said to His disciples:

> "When I sent you out with no purse or bag or sandals, did you lack anything?" They said, "Nothing." He said to them, "But now, let him who has a purse take it, and likewise a bag. And let him who has no sword sell his mantle and buy one. For I tell you that this scripture must be fulfilled in Me, 'And he was reckoned with transgressors.'" (Lk 22:35-37)

Why this change? Why suddenly put the disciples on guard against the hostility they will encounter? Jesus knew that according to the Scriptures, the gospel would be preached to the end of the earth. The Good News was first announced to the Jews, but they rejected it, as St John tells us in the prologue to his Gospel: the Word "came to his own home, and his own people received Him not . . ." (Jn 1:11). The Cross was the consequence of this refusal: Jesus had to be "lifted up" on the wood so that, as He said, "I will draw all men to Myself" (Jn 12:32). After the Resurrection He tells His disciples, "You shall be My witnesses in Jerusalem and in all Judea and Samaria and to the end of the earth" (Acts 1:8). "Go therefore and make disciples of all nations, baptizing them in the name of the Father and of the Son and of the Holy Spirit, teaching them to observe all that I have commanded you. And lo, I am with you always, to the close of the age" (Mt 28:19-20). Jesus knew that if "His own" rejected the Word, the world would resist the gospel with even greater force. That is why He warned His disciples that they would encounter many difficulties: ". . . the kingdom of heaven has suffered violence, and men of violence take it by force" (Mt 11:12).

The gospel has been preached for two thousand years and the Good News has been spread to the ends of the earth, but the world still resists its message. It is rejected not only by the external world but also by our interior world. Only those of us who destroy the old self and accept the Cross will be able to enter into the Kingdom of God. The Savior's Cross stands as an eternal symbol of the struggle against evil to which the disciples of the crucified and risen One are called, in order to hasten the Day of His victorious Second Coming.

G) ". . . all Israel will be saved . . ." (Rom 11:26)

As we have seen, the Lord Himself foretold that "Jerusalem will be trodden down by the Gentiles [non-Jews], until the times of the Gentiles are fulfilled" (Lk 21:24). Thus we are told that Israel will return to the Kingdom. These words of the Lord are explained by the apostle Paul in the Epistle to the Romans:

> I want you to understand this mystery, brethren: a hardening has come upon part of Israel, until the full number of the Gentiles come in, and so all Israel will be saved . . . (Rom 11:25-26)

After the gospel has been preached to the whole world—and this seems to have been accomplished, at least on the horizontal, geographical plane[8]—the "time of the Gentiles" will come to an end, and the Jews will be admitted into the Church, as St Paul tells us. "And so all Israel will be saved" and "the Deliverer will come from Zion . . ." (Rom 11:26).

8. See page 347.

H) ". . . the man of lawlessness is revealed, the son of perdition . . ." (2 Thess 2:3)

The last sign to appear before the end of the world is the Antichrist, the embodiment of all the injustice and evil of which we have spoken.

Although Jesus did not use the term antichrist, He alluded to it in a reference to the prophecy of Daniel:

"So when you see the desolating sacrilege spoken of by the prophet Daniel standing in the holy place . . . then let those who are in Judea flee to the mountains . . ." (Mt 24:15-16)

And St Paul says in the First Epistle to Timothy (4:1-2):

Now the Spirit expressly says that in later times some will depart from the faith by giving heed to deceitful spirits and doctrines of demons, through the pretensions of liars whose consciences are seared . . .

And he continues in the Second Epistle to the Thessalonians:

Now concerning the coming of our Lord Jesus Christ . . . we beg you, brethren, not to be quickly shaken in mind or excited either by spirit or by word . . . to the effect that the day of the Lord has come. Let no one deceive you in any way. For that day will not come, unless the rebellion[9] comes first, and the man of lawlessness is revealed, the son of perdition, who opposes and exalts himself against every so-called god or object of worship, so that he takes his seat in the temple of God, proclaiming himself to be God . . . And then the lawless one will be revealed, and the Lord Jesus will slay him with the breath of His mouth and destroy him by His appearing and His coming. The coming of the lawless one by the activity of Satan will be with all power and with pretended signs and wonders, and with all wicked deception for those who are to perish, because they refused to love the truth and so be saved. (2 Thess 2:1-4, 8-10)

9. Apostasy is a Greek word which means secession, defection, or denial.

This is the beast which is described in the Apocalypse.

> The whole earth followed the beast with wonder . . . And the beast
> was given a mouth uttering haughty and blasphemous words, . . .
> it opened its mouth to utter blasphemies against God . . . Also it
> was allowed to make war on the saints and to conquer them. And
> authority was given it over every tribe and people and tongue and
> nation . . . Here is a call for the endurance and faith of the saints.
> (Rev 13:3, 5-7, 10)

In his first two epistles, St John gives the name of antichrist to
the "destroyer" of the Book of Daniel, to St Paul's "son of perdition,"
and to the "beast" of Revelation.

> Who is the liar but he who denies that Jesus is the Christ?
> This is the antichrist, he who denies the Father and the Son.
> (1 Jn 2:22)

> . . . and every spirit which does not confess Jesus is not of God.
> This is the spirit of antichrist, of which you heard that it was
> coming, and now it is in the world already. (1 Jn 4:3)

> . . . as you have heard that antichrist is coming, so now many
> antichrists have come; therefore we know that it is the last hour.
> (1 Jn 2:18)

> . . . many deceivers have gone out into the world, men who will
> not acknowledge the coming of Jesus Christ in the flesh; such a
> one is the deceiver and the antichrist. (2 Jn 7)

Seeker: These texts of St John make it sound like antichrist has
already come.

Sage: No, St John is here speaking of the servants of antichrist,
the "deceivers" who have manifested the spirit of antichrist (men
like Nero or Hitler). Some have already come and others will follow,
but the son of perdition, *the* Antichrist, will only appear shortly
before the Day of the Lord.*

---

*Thus the Antichrist is a tool of Satan and is not the Devil incarnate. See also the Synaxarion
for Meat-fare Sunday.

Seeker: So we expect Satan before Christ?"

Sage: Don't be afraid. "The Lord Jesus will slay him with the breath of His mouth and destroy him by His appearing and His coming" (2 Thess 2:8). But be vigilant. Don't let yourself be seduced by the Liar who will imitate Christ so that he may deceive us more easily. Arm yourself with hope and faith so that evil and the temporary triumphs of the wicked do not discourage you. The Lord Himself says, "Fear not, little flock, for it is your Father's good pleasure to give you the kingdom" (Lk 12:32).

CHAPTER 34

THE END OF THE WORLD
AND THE CREATION OF THE NEW WORLD

A) The End of the World

Biblical revelation teaches us that this world has a beginning and an end.[10] This idea can be traced through the whole Bible. "'I am the Alpha and the Omega,' says the Lord God, who is and who was and who is to come, the Almighty" (Rev 1:8).

In the Old Testament

The end of the world is first mentioned in Ps 101:26-28 [102:25-27]:

> Of old Thou didst lay the foundation of the earth, and the heavens are the work of Thy hands. They will perish, but Thou dost endure; they will all wear out like a garment. Thou changest them like a raiment, and they pass away; but Thou art the same, and Thy years have no end.

We find the same idea, expressed in almost the same words, in Isaiah:

> . . . the heavens will vanish like smoke, the earth will wear out like a garment, and they who dwell in it will die like gnats; but My salvation will be for ever, and My deliverance will never be ended." (Is 51:6)

And he describes even more explicitly how

> . . . the earth is utterly broken, the earth is rent asunder, the earth is violently shaken. The earth staggers like a drunken man, it sways

10. See part I, as well as Gen 1:1; 2 Macc 7:28; Pss 32 [33]; 103 [104]; 18 [19].

like a hut; its transgression lies heavy upon it, and it falls, and will not rise again. . . . Then the moon will be confounded, and the sun ashamed . . . (Is 24:19-20,23)

And further:

All the host of heaven shall rot away, and the skies roll up like a scroll. All their host shall fall, as leaves fall from the vine, like leaves falling from the fig tree. (Is 34:4)

The prophet Joel foretells the same thing: "The sun and the moon are darkened, and the stars withdraw their shining" (Joel 2:10; 4:15).

In the New Testament

The New Testament uses the same imagery but goes into greater detail. The Lord Jesus says, "Immediately after the tribulation of those days the sun will be darkened, and the moon will not give its light, and the stars will fall from heaven, and the powers of the heavens will be shaken . . ." (Mt 24:29; Mk 13:24-25; Lk 21:25-26).

The apostle Peter picks up the same theme:

But by the same word the heavens and earth that now exist have been stored up for fire, being kept until the day of judgment and destruction of ungodly men . . . But the day of the Lord will come like the thief, and then the heavens will pass away with a loud noise, and the elements will be dissolved with fire, and the earth and the works that are upon it will be burned up . . . The heavens will be kindled and dissolved, and the elements will melt with fire! (2 Pet 3:7, 10, 12)

St John describes the same scene in the Book of Revelation: "from His presence earth and sky fled away, and no place was found for them" (Rev 20:11). "The first heaven and the first earth passed away, and the sea was no more" (Rev 21:1).

B) The New World

Seeker: The Bible tells us that after the Flood "God promised that 'never again shall all flesh be cut off by the waters of a flood,' and never again shall there be a flood[11] to destroy the earth" (Gen 9:11). But what the New Testament foretells is far worse than the Flood.

Sage: The world continued to exist after the Flood because the Flood was meant to destroy evil and not the earth itself. God warned us of the consequences of evil, but He didn't break the Covenant. Hope, symbolized by the dove, was rekindled by the salvation of Noah and all those who sought refuge in the ark. The New Testament texts foretell the final destruction of this world. It's natural to be afraid. But mustn't the *old* world disappear before the *new* one can be established, a world initiated by Christ's earthly ministry and fulfilled by His Second Coming? It will certainly be a terrible day for the godless who will be destroyed (2 Pet 3:7-12). But it will also be a day of glory which we are eagerly awaiting, for on that day Christ "delivers the kingdom to God the Father after destroying every rule and every authority and power" (1 Cor 15:24). On that day a new world of which Isaiah speaks will be created by God. "For behold, I create new heavens and a new earth; and the former things shall not be remembered or come to mind" (Is 65:17). And the apostle Peter writes, "But according to His promise we wait for new heavens and a new earth in which righteousness dwells" (2 Pet 3:13). Finally, St John exclaims in Revelation, "Then I saw a new heaven and a new earth" (Rev 21:1), and he hears the Lord saying, "Behold, I make all things new" (Rev. 21:5).

Don't be afraid of death or the end of the world, just as you're not afraid of the night. You know that day will follow. Remember that since you are baptized, you're already living in the new world which is to come: "If any one is in Christ, he is a new creation; the old has passed away, behold, the new has come" (2 Cor 5:17). He is a new creature, dead to sin, re-born in God. Listen to what St Paul says: "For you have died, and your life is hid with Christ in God. When Christ who is our life appears, then you also will appear with Him in glory" (Col 3:3-4). The Lord will come and the dead will rise bodily into eternal life.

---

11. See chapter 8, p. 97, and chapter 15, p. 221.

CHAPTER 35

THE RESURRECTION OF THE DEAD

Is the resurrection of the flesh a reality? Or is it a myth which embodies an outdated and unreasonable belief?

When Peter came down from the upper room into the streets of Jerusalem, illumined by the fire of the Holy Spirit, he proclaimed the risen Christ (Acts 2:14-36). He referred to the Scriptures, citing Psalm 15[16]:9-11: "Therefore my heart is glad, and my soul rejoices; my body also dwells secure. For Thou dost not give me up to Sheol, or let Thy godly one see the Pit. Thou dost show me the path of life . . ." The apostle explained that David, the author of the psalm, "both died and was buried, and his tomb is with us to this day. Being therefore a prophet, and knowing that God had sworn with an oath to him that He would set one of his descendants upon his throne, he foresaw and spoke of the resurrection of Christ" (Acts 2:29-31). Thus it is Jesus Christ, the descendant of David and vanquisher of death, our "incorruptible Pascha," who gives the hope of resurrection to all flesh. We are referring specifically to the resurrection of the flesh. It is very concrete. It is not an abstract notion in which the soul survives outside the fleshly shell, purified so that it may live in a disembodied world of "ideas," as some philosophers teach us. Both the psalmist and Peter place all their hopes in the salvation of the flesh from corruption.

Seeker: What is corruption?
Sage: Corruption is the decomposition of the body, its return into the earth. Remember the story of Creation (Gen 2:7). Man was taken from the earth and to the earth he returns, because after the Fall evil, suffering, death and corruption were introduced into God's beautiful creation. "You shall return to the ground, for out of it you were taken; you are dust, and to dust you shall return" (Gen 3:19).

Nevertheless we believe and hope that the dead will live again. "I look for the resurrection of the dead and the life of the world to come," are the last words of the Creed.

Seeker: How can that be? I have trouble believing that the dead will live again.

Sage: Let's hold very closely to the texts so as not to deviate from the true faith. In this mysterious realm of death and resurrection we should not invent or assert anything on our own. We must avoid an unhealthy curiosity which seeks to communicate with the other world, or to learn the secrets of the dead.[12] Only the Scriptures can reveal the truth, for the Holy Spirit "who spoke by the prophets" teaches us through them. So let's look through the Bible for texts which speak of the resurrection of the flesh.

A) *In the Old Testament*

When man dies he returns to the dust. Nevertheless the prophet Daniel promises, "And many of those who sleep in the dust of the earth shall awake, some to everlasting life, and some to shame and everlasting contempt" (Dan 12:2).

Isaiah expresses the same hope: "Thy dead shall live, their bodies shall rise. O dwellers in the dust, awake and sing for joy! For Thy dew is a dew of light, and on the land of the shades Thou wilt let it fall" (Is 26:19). It is like a second birth, a re-creation.

Job, an innocent man in agony, abandoned and suffering on a dunghill, cries out, "I know that my Redeemer lives, and at last He will stand upon the earth; and after my skin has been thus destroyed, then from my flesh I shall see God" (Jb 19:25-26). Job knows that he will see God with the eyes of the flesh and we share this belief. The dunghill is our fallen world, we are surrounded by corruption and death; nevertheless we proclaim that we will see God. Jonah, in the belly of the great fish, which represents hell, knows that God can hear him. "Out of the belly of Sheol I cried, and Thou didst hear my voice" (Jon 2:2). Jesus uses the words of Jonah to answer un-

---

12. See for example Lev 19:31: "Do not turn to mediums or wizards; do not seek them out, to be defiled by them."

believers who look for proofs and guarantees. The sign of Jonah is hope in the resurrection, hope when everything seems lost, when we seem to be in hell, when everything seems hopeless. "For as Jonah was three days and three nights in the belly of the whale, so will the Son of man be three days and three nights in the heart of the earth" (Mt 12:40).

Seeker: I believe that Christ, the Son of God, could not stay in the tomb because He's God, the Source of life. It's logical that He should rise from the dead. But the resurrection of the flesh doesn't make sense in our case!

Sage: The Resurrection of Christ is not as obvious or logical as you say. It is incomprehensible and amazing that the Son of God should possess a human body in reality and not just in appearance. But He did! He is not a spirit who, for a limited time, appeared in human form. (This is the heresy of docetism.) If this were true, Jesus would have experienced death without really being touched by it, because He had never possessed a physical body. "See My hands and My feet, that it is I Myself; handle Me, and see; for a spirit has not flesh and bones as you see that I have" (Lk 24:39), Jesus says to His apostles after the Resurrection. And to show that He is really alive, He eats in front of them (Lk 24:39-43).

St Paul correctly calls Jesus the first-born from the dead (Col 1:18). He arose, not only for Himself—it was not a selfish experiment performed to amaze mankind—but that all people, all flesh, might arise following Him. All flesh, even decomposed flesh, will return to life, for what God has created in His image cannot disintegrate into nothingness. The prophecy of Ezekiel which we chant during matins of Great and Holy Saturday affirms this resurrection. Let's read this text, one of the most striking in the Old Testament, in its entirety.

> The hand of the Lord was upon me, and He brought me out by the Spirit of the Lord, and set me down in the midst of the valley; it was full of bones. And He led me round among them; and behold, there were very many upon the valley; and lo, they were very dry. And He said to me, "Son of man, can these bones live?" And I answered, "O Lord God, Thou knowest." Again He said to me,

"Prophesy to these bones, and say to them, O dry bones, hear the word of the Lord. Thus says the Lord God to these bones: Behold, I will cause breath to enter you, and you shall live. And I will lay sinews upon you, and will cause flesh to come upon you and cover you with skin, and put breath in you, and you shall live; and you shall know that I am the Lord."

So I prophesied as I was commanded. And as I prophesied, there was a noise, and behold, a rattling; and the bones came together, bone to its bone. And as I looked, there were sinews on them, and flesh had come upon them, and skin had covered them; but there was no breath in them. Then He said to me, "Prophesy to the breath, prophesy, son of man, and say to the breath, Thus says the Lord God: Come from the four winds, O breath, and breathe upon these slain, that they may live." So I prophesied as He commanded me, and the breath came into them, and they lived, and stood upon their feet, an exceedingly great host.

Then He said to me, "Son of man, these bones are the whole house of Israel. Behold, they say, 'Our bones are dried up, and our hope is lost; we are clean cut off.' Therefore prophesy, and say to them, Thus says the Lord God: Behold, I will open your graves, and raise you from your graves, O My people; and I will bring you home into the land of Israel. And you shall know that I am the Lord, when I open your graves, and raise you from your graves, O My people. And I will put My Spirit within you, and you shall live, and I will place you in your own land; then you shall know that I, the Lord, have spoken, and I have done it, says the Lord." (Ezek 37:1-14)

During the canon of the burial service we sing,

For out of the earth were we mortals made,
and unto the same earth shall we return again,
as Thou didst command when Thou madest me, saying unto me:
For dust thou art, and unto dust shalt thou return.
Whither we mortals all shall go,
making our lamentation the song:
Alleluia! Alleluia! Alleluia!

How could we sing alleluia from the dust, unless like Job, Jonah, and the three youths in the furnace, we had hope of life even in the abyss of death?

B) In the New Testament

Jesus Himself confirms us in this hope. In a passage now read during the funeral service, He has promised that we will hear His voice: "Truly, truly, I say to you, the hour is coming, and now is, when the dead will hear the voice of the Son of God, and those who hear will live . . . The hour is coming when all who are in the tombs will hear His voice and come forth" (Jn 5:25, 28-29).

St Paul recalls this promise in the first Epistle to the Thessalonians, which is also read at the burial service:

> But we would not have you ignorant, brethren, concerning those who are asleep, that you may not grieve as others do who have no hope. For since we believe that Jesus died and rose again, even so, through Jesus, God will bring with Him those who have fallen asleep. For this we declare to you by the word of the Lord, that we who are alive, who are left until the coming of the Lord, shall not precede those who have fallen asleep. For the Lord Himself will descend from heaven with a cry of command, with the archangel's call, and with the sound of the trumpet of God. And the dead in Christ will rise first; then we who are alive, who are left, shall be caught up together with them in the clouds to meet the Lord in the air; and so we shall always be with the Lord. Therefore comfort one another with these words. (1 Thess 4:13-18)

Seeker: Doesn't the soul alone go to the Lord? During the burial service we sing over and over, "Grant rest to the soul of Thy servant who has fallen asleep." Doesn't that mean that the body and soul are separated and the body is put in the tomb and returns to dust?

Sage: St Irenaeus, Bishop of Lyons during the latter part of the second century, in his youth a disciple of Polycarp who had himself been a disciple of the evangelist John, has a striking answer to this question: "If Christ did not save the body and the flesh in the resurrection, He would not save man at all, for who has ever seen a man without a body."

All too often we over-simplify human reality by opposing its fleshly side to the spiritual side, seeing man as a duality at war with himself. The flesh,[13] we think, is subject to evil and doomed to corruption while the soul, delivered from its corporeal prison, is purified. Only the soul can be saved and share in God's eternity. This puritanical attitude gives rise to a distrust of everything fleshly. We put everything fleshly on one side and everything spiritual on the other. The body is part of the corrupt material world, while the soul belongs to the spiritual realm. The flesh is impure, while the soul aspires to purity. The body, we suppose, is earthly, the soul celestial.

But God created the whole person. The body becomes evil only if the spirit turns away from God through sin and uses it to enslave the soul.

Of course, we do read in St. Paul, "Wretched man that I am! Who will deliver me from this body of death?" (Rom 7:24). And again, "To set the mind on the flesh is death, but to set the mind on the Spirit is life and peace. For the mind that is set on the flesh is hostile to God" (Rom 8:6-7). But does that mean that St. Paul despises the flesh? Certainly not, for he knows that the flesh is saved and glorified by Christ's victory over death. "The body is . . . meant . . . for the Lord, and the Lord for the body. And God raised the Lord and will also raise us up by His power. Do you not know that your bodies are members of Christ? . . . He who is united to the Lord becomes one spirit with Him . . . Do you not know that your body is a temple of the Holy Spirit . . . So glorify God in your body" (1 Cor 6:13-15, 17, 19, 20). And further: "For in Him the whole fulness of deity dwells bodily, and you have come to fulness of life in Him" (Col 2:9-10).

Of course, if the spirit becomes enslaved by the body, man is dragged down into materialism and his spirit is shackled by inertia: "Watch and pray that you may not enter into temptation; the spirit indeed is willing, but the flesh is weak" (Mt 26:41). The body is not the source of evil, but it can become the instrument of sin, "the sinful body." However, Jesus Christ our Savior has crucified the old man

---

13. The word "flesh" is used in the Bible to express the fragility of man. In the New Testament, the word specifically refers to a humanity disfigured by sin.

(Rom 6:6) and delivered us from slavery by assuming our body. "For as by a man came death, by a man has come also the resurrection of the dead. For as in Adam all die, so also in Christ shall all be made alive (1 Cor 15:21-22). Thus St Paul reveals a great mystery: our body becomes the bearer of the Holy Spirit and our whole being is transformed. The flesh of us all can become immortal because it has been assumed by Jesus and made spiritual by His Spirit. "If the Spirit of Him who raised Jesus from the dead dwells in you, He who raised Christ Jesus from the dead will give life to your mortal bodies also through His Spirit which dwells in you" (Rom 8:11).

> When the perishable puts on the imperishable, and the mortal puts on immortality, then shall come to pass the saying that is written: "Death is swallowed up in victory." "O death, where is thy victory? O death, where is thy sting?" . . . But thanks be to God, who gives us the victory through our Lord Jesus Christ. (1 Cor 15:54-55, 57)

CHAPTER 36

LITURGICAL TIME

Seeker: You say that the resurrection of the dead will occur when the Lord returns on the day of His Second Coming. But what happens to us *after* the death and burial of our body now, *before* the resurrection of the flesh?

Sage: During our earthly life we live in the body and perceive reality through the five senses. That is why our experience is spatially limited. We think of time as if it were a line moving forward from point to point, from A to Z. Our language is an expression of this way of thinking and feeling; it is full of words like "before," "after," "yesterday," and "tomorrow."[14]

Christ, who is both God and man, allows us to participate in another reality which passes beyond the limits of space and time. We find this idea in the Holy Scriptures: "A thousand years in Thy sight are but as yesterday when it is past" says Psalm 89 [90]; and St Peter continues, "with the Lord one day is as a thousand years, and a thousand years as one day" (2 Pet 3:8). The psalmist and St Peter use human language because we cannot understand any other. The point is not that 1000 years = 1 day and vice versa; this is not a mathematical equation (which is still within the limits of space and time). What we are dealing with is the idea that there is no common measure between human time and God's eternity. It is not that eternity is the "opposite" of time; it is simply a completely different reality. Jesus Himself hints at this when He says to the Jews, "Before Abraham was, I am" (Jn 8:58). Within divine reality "yesterday" and "tomorrow" are somehow present in "today" (or this day "which the Lord has made"). It is not a point between "before"

---

14. Among certain Orientals, there is found another experience of time, consisting of "leaving" space and linear time. But this approach is alien to the average Westerner.

and "after" but a recapitulation of everything in God. "Today" is not time at a standstill; God is life ("I am who I am" [Ex 3:14]) and therefore cannot be static. His life is not defined by birth and death as ours is; it is eternal life. Eternal life should not be defined as time without end; it cannot be measured in human categories derived from our physical experiences.

We can participate in this reality which surpasses space and time even here on earth, because according to Christ's promise, "where two or three are gathered in My name, there am I in the midst of them" (Mt 18:20). This is especially true during the Eucharist, because we then receive the whole Christ. "He who eats My flesh and drinks My blood abides in Me, and I in Him" (Jn 6:56).

Christ lived in history, in our linear time. But He ascended into heaven and sits in glory at the right hand of the Father. Again, this "right hand of the Father" should not be understood as a place measurable by scientific instruments. It is a "place" outside our definition of space. And from this "place" He shall come to judge the living and the dead. The Christ of whom we become a part is He whom the celestial powers serve and in whom all the saints, the dead and the living, are united in communion. When we come to church to be united in the eucharistic community around our bishop, we bring as an offering the fruits of the earth and of our labor, and also everything that God has given us. This includes all our fellow men, for whom we Christians bear responsibility. However, even though we participate in a reality which surpasses space and time, we do not reject history. When we sing, "now let us lay aside all earthly cares," we do not mean that the world and its history no longer concern us. It means that we make an offering of our time, which we no longer consider only in its purely human, limited dimension, in the way of "this world." In the encounter of human time and divine eternity during the Liturgy, there emerges a new reality of time and space ("Behold, I make all things new" [Rev 21:5]). This means that everything becomes possible: we are no longer limited by the laws of nature and historical chance. Miracles become possible because in this encounter of time and eternity the Kingdom is already mysteriously present, even though it will be revealed in its fullness only later.

And what about the dead who "await" the resurrection? We don't know what waiting means for those who are outside the realm of space and time and who are "in the bosom of Abraham." At least let's not invent stories, as so often is done, by applying our categories of space and time to the beyond.

What we do know is that at the Liturgy the dead are present, together with the saints and heavenly powers, and that we pray for them and with them. That's what we mean when we say that in the Liturgy we are in communion with the saints. Also, let's not forget that, as St John Chrysostom says, every time we celebrate the eucharistic liturgy, we are celebrating Holy Pascha. That is to say, we participate in the Resurrection to which we must bear witness, both in our lives and to the world.

CHAPTER 37

LIFE IN DEATH

A) What is Death?

This is a fundamental question which we must now ask ourselves. Psalm 103 [104] gives us our first answer. We already know from Genesis (2:7) that the divine breath is the source of human life: "the Lord God formed man of dust from the ground, and breathed into his nostrils the breath of life; and man became a living being." Thus the life of those created "in the image and likeness of God" (Gen 1:26) is closely linked to our Creator. Psalm 103 [104] draws the obvious conclusion that when the divine breath is withdrawn, death follows: "When Thou hidest Thy face, they are dismayed; when Thou takest away their breath, they die and return to their dust" (v. 29).

Nevertheless, man's death is *against nature,* for "God created man for incorruption, and made him in the image of His own eternity" (Wis 2:23). Man was created for life and not for death: "because God did not make death, and He does not delight in the death of the living" (Wis 1:13). The link between the body and life, between the body and soul, is so natural[15] that we cannot imagine life without a body.

But through the devil's envy death entered the world, and those who belong to his party experience it" (Wis 2:24). St Paul takes up the same idea: "For the wages of sin is death . . . sin came into the world through one man and death through sin" (Rom 6:23; 5:12). By turning away from the Source of life at the instigation of "him who has the power of death, that is, the devil" (Heb 2:14), man has cut himself off from Life and put himself into a situation where death, the disintegration of human nature, is triumphant.

15. This is expressed in the funeral liturgy.

Seeker: I would like to come back to my original question: What happens to us after the death and burial of our body, before the resurrection of the flesh?

Sage: The best way to answer is to review all the stages of revelation in relation to this question.

B) *The Dead According to the Psalms and the Prophets*

The psalms and ancient prophets describe death or Sheol as "silence," "the land of forgetfulness," "dust," "the abyss."

> For in death there is no remembrance of Thee; in Sheol who can give Thee praise? (Ps 6:6[5])

> What profit is there in my death, if I go down to the Pit? Will the dust praise Thee? Will it tell of Thy faithfulness? (Ps 29:10 [30:9])

> Dost Thou work wonders for the dead? Do the shades rise up to praise Thee? Is Thy steadfast love declared in the grave or Thy faithfulness in Abaddon? Are Thy wonders known in the darkness, or Thy saving help in the land of forgetfulness? (Ps 87:11-13 [88:10-12])

> The dead do not praise the Lord, nor do any that go down into silence. (Ps 113:25 [115:17])

> For Sheol cannot thank Thee, death cannot praise Thee; those who go down to the pit cannot hope for Thy faithfulness. (Is 38:18)

Thus the ancient prophets saw death as a state of perdition, silence, and forgetfulness. The dead are "asleep." And yet the hope of resurrection is already being expressed. We find it in Psalm 15 [16], cited by Peter in Acts; we find it in the Book of Isaiah (26:19); and even more clearly it appears in the Books of Job (19:25-26) and Ezekiel (37:9-14). The author of the Book of Daniel also contrasts the sleep of death with the awakening of the resurrection which is to come (Dan 12:2).

C) The Death of the Just in the Book of Wisdom

The last books of the Old Testament[16] reveal a new aspect of the life after death, an aspect which will be more clearly defined in the New Testament. This teaching as expressed in the Book of Wisdom has greatly influenced the thinking of the Church.

> But the righteous man, though he die early, will be at rest. (Wis 4:7)

> But the souls of the righteous are in the hand of God,[17] and no torment will ever touch them. In the eyes of the foolish they seemed to have died, and their departure was thought to be an affliction, and their going from us to be their destruction; but they are at peace . . . God tested them and found them worthy of Himself; like gold in the furnace He tried them, and like a sacrificial burnt offering He accepted them. In the time of their visitation they will shine forth . . . Those who trust in Him will understand truth, and the faithful will abide with Him in love, because grace and mercy are upon His elect, and He watches over His holy ones. (Wis 3:1-3,5-7,9)

> But the righteous live for ever, and their reward is with the Lord:[18] the Most High takes care of them. Therefore they will receive a glorious crown and a beautiful diadem[19] from the hand of the Lord. (Wis 5:15-16)

Thus the Book of Wisdom makes a distinction between those among the dead: the just only seem to die; their lives are actually in the hand of God. They live eternally.

---

16. This refers to books which were written in Greek during the 150 years preceding the birth of Christ—particularly the Book of Wisdom and the Second Book of Maccabees. On Maccabees, see chapter 39, p. 379, note 30.
17. Much earlier, Moses had already said to God: "Yea, he loved his peoples; all those consecrated to him were *in his hand*" (Deut 33:3).
18. See also Ps 72 [73]:24: "Thou wilt receive me to glory."
19. Isaiah had already proclaimed that God's salvation is "to all generations" (Is 51:8).

D) *Eternal Life in the New Testament*

Hope is transformed into certainty by the coming of Life itself in the Person of our Lord Jesus Christ. Using the image of "the hand of God" found in the Book of Wisdom, the Lord Jesus says in the Gospel of John:

> My sheep hear My voice, . . . I give them eternal life, and they shall never perish, and no one shall snatch them out of My hand. (10:27-28)

> For this is the will of My Father, that every one who sees the Son and believes in Him should have eternal life; and I will raise him up at the last day . . . Truly, truly, I say to you, he who believes in Me has eternal life. (6:40, 47)

> Truly, truly, I say to you, if any one keeps My word, he will never see death. (8:51)

> . . . he who believes in Me, though he die, yet shall he live, and whoever lives and believes in Me shall never die. (11:25-26)

Man continues to live[20]—even after the death of his body—in proportion to the degree to which he is united to God. That is why Jesus says in the Gospel of St Matthew, "do not fear those who kill the body but cannot kill the soul; rather fear Him who can destroy both soul and body in hell" (10:28). Then are death and hell the absence of God, the place or condition where God is not? The soul which thirsts for God and seeks His presence will not perish, for the longing for God will keep it alive. Furthermore, he who lives in Christ in this world continues to live in Christ even after leaving the body.

St Paul affirms this with absolute certainty:

> For we know that if the earthly tent we live in is destroyed, we have a building from God, a house not made with hands, eternal

---

20. The Greek word *psyche* can be translated either as "soul" or "life." Biblical texts suggest a meaning of "life," which God gives to those near Him. The notion of the soul as a constituent "part" of the person derives more from Greek philosophy than biblical revelation.

The Descent into Hades

With the Saints Give Rest

Kievan Chant

With the Saints give rest, O Christ, to the soul(s) of Thy ser - - vant(s), where sick - ness and sor - row are no more, nei - ther sigh - ing, but life ev - er - last - ing.

in the heavens. Here indeed we groan, and long to put on our heavenly dwelling, so that by putting it on we may not be found naked . . . So we are always of good courage; we know that while we are at home in the body we are away from the Lord . . . We are of good courage, and we would rather be away from the body and at home with the Lord. (2 Cor 5:1-3, 6, 8)

St Paul expresses the same faith—the same certainty that he will live in Christ beyond the death of his body—in the Epistle to the Phillippians: "it is my eager expectation and hope that I shall not be at all ashamed . . . For me to live is Christ, and to die is gain . . . My desire is to depart and be with Christ . . ." (Phil 1:20-21, 23).

Christ is life because He is God, the Giver of Life. (in Greek, *zoodotis*[21]). One who lives in Christ, whose life is "hid with Christ in God" (Col 3:3), has "memory eternal,"[22] for he is sustained by the Spirit of God and death has no hold over him. "When Christ who is our life appears, then you also will appear with Him in glory" (Col 3:4).

Seeker: You're talking about those who live in Christ, but what about all the others, those who died before the coming of Christ or those today who don't believe in Him? What happens to them after death?

Sage: The apostle Peter answers your question: ". . . He [Christ] went and preached to the spirits in prison, who formerly did not obey, when God's patience waited in the days of Noah, during the building of the ark . . ." (1 Pet 3:19-20).

Those who were, are, or will be rebels, become "spirits in prison" after death. They are in Sheol, the "place of perdition," the "land of forgetfulness," of which the psalms and Isaiah spoke. The Lord Jesus Himself uses striking imagery to describe the fate of the rebel in the parable of Lazarus and the rich man. The rich man "died and was buried; and in Hades,[23] being in torment, he lifted up his eyes,

---

21. *Zoodotis:* Greek word derived from *zoe* = life, and *dotes* = giver.
22. Ps 111 [112], taken up in the funeral liturgy.
23. Christ also speaks of this "dwelling-place of the dead," of this "Sheol," of this "Hades," regarding Capernaum: "And you, Capernaum, will you be exalted to heaven? You shall be brought down to Hades" (Mt 11:23).

and saw Abraham far off and Lazarus in his bosom. And he called out, 'Father Abraham, have mercy upon me, and send Lazarus to dip the end of his finger in water and cool my tongue; for I am in anguish in this flame'" (Lk 16:22-24).

This Hades is separated from the "land of the living," the "bosom of Abraham," the "place of brightness,"[24] by a great abyss so that, as Abraham explains, "those who would pass from here to you may not be able, and none may cross from there to us" (Lk 16:26).

But "what is impossible with men is possible with God" (Lk 18:27). And Christ, God made man, descends from heaven, not only down to earth but also into the abyss. He looks for us in the lowest depths,[25] even in Sheol or hell, so that He might break the eternal bonds, liberate Adam and Eve from their prison, and allow those who hear His voice to participate in "the resurrection of Life" which had been promised to the just who accept His love. This is what the icon of the Resurrection represents. Notice the extraordinary power of the Risen One "trampling down death by death and upon those in the tombs bestowing life."

Now we can understand Christ's dialogue with the Good Thief. As soon as the criminal acquires the faith to discern the royalty of the dying Man crucified at his side, together with enough hope to dare ask Him, "Remember me, O Lord, when Thou comest into Thy Kingdom," Jesus answers, "Today you will be with Me in Paradise." Whoever believes that "with God all things are possible" (Mt 19:26) and places himself confidently in the hands of Christ the Savior, will find himself with Christ in Paradise at the moment of his physical death, in "a house not made with hands, eternal in the heavens" (2 Cor 5:1), in joyous anticipation of the Resurrection.

24. This concerns those who are in the "hand of God."
25. Cf. also Eph 4:9; Phil 2:10.

CHAPTER 38

THE LAST JUDGMENT

A) Divine Justice in This World and the Next

Seeker: Since even criminals can be saved, and since Christ has freed the prisoners of hell, does that mean that there's no eternal punishment?

Sage: No, there is. Although God is infinitely merciful, He is also perfectly just. To us, justice and mercy often seem irreconcilable. But God, "who tries the heart and the mind" (Jer 11:20 and Ps 7:10 [9]) is able to manifest infinite mercy and absolute justice at the same time. The possibility of eternal punishment is not excluded simply because the worst criminals can receive forgiveness and salvation. Only God can judge; "for we know Him who said, 'Vengeance is Mine, I will repay.' . . . It is a fearful thing to fall into the hands of the living God" (Heb 10:30-31; Deut 32:35).

Seeker: You want to scare me, to make me feel guilty! Hell-fire, devils with pitchforks, that's silly now! That's all in the past, now everything is permitted!

Sage: Don't debase God's justice and confuse it with popular imagery and mythical representations of the Middle Ages. If, as you say, there is a tendency in our society to make everything, including crime, acceptable, does that mean that God should "allow" even torturers into His Kingdom to continue their sinister activities? No, He waits for their repentance. Do you think that He will allow tyrants to exploit and torture the innocent indefinitely? Do you think that He doesn't hear the cries of martyrs who, as St John tells us, call out, "O Sovereign Lord, holy and true, how long before Thou wilt judge and avenge our blood on those who dwell upon the earth?" (Rev 6:10)? No, for "behold, I judge between sheep and sheep, rams and he-goats . . . I will save My flock, they shall no longer be a prey;

and I will judge between sheep and sheep" (Ezek 34:17,22). God's justice is the work of salvation; His punishment frees the innocent and saves the victims. "He put on righteousness as a breastplate, and a helmet of salvation upon His head" (Is 59:17). We can then say, glory to God who delivers the oppressed and removes tyrants (the Herods, the Neros, the Hitlers) from their thrones.

At first the prophets see judgment as God's intervention in this world when He saves His faithful servants who submit to trials and persecution with the patience of Job. He saves them and punishes the tyrants; "then once more you shall distinguish between the righteous and the wicked" (Mal 3:18). The Lord's Day, of which the prophets speak (Amos 5:18-20; Is 13:6-9; Jer 46:10), assures the ruin of sinners and the liberation and triumph of the just. Sooner or later, God's justice manifests itself. The whole Book of Psalms and all the prophets bear witness to the expectation of God's justice.

> But the wicked perish; the enemies of the Lord are like the glory of the pastures, they vanish, like smoke they vanish away . . . The righteous shall possess the land and dwell upon it forever. (Ps 36 [37]: 20, 29)

That is why on the night of the Resurrection, when the Lord appears to us, we sing,

> Let God arise, let His enemies be scattered; let those who hate Him flee before Him! As smoke is driven away, so drive them away; as wax melts before fire, let the wicked perish before God! But let the righteous be joyful; let them exult before God; let them be jubilant with joy! (Ps 67:2-4 [61:1-3])

Seeker: Nevertheless, the wicked still prosper and get rich while the righteous suffer and live in misery.

Sage: The prophet Jeremiah was aware of that long before you. "Why does the way of the wicked prosper? Why do all who are treacherous thrive?" he asks (Jer 12:1). But divine justice is apparent even in this world. The prosperity of the wicked is only temporary. Biblical and even secular history bear witness to this. Divine justice manifests itself in this world through many spectacular signs such as the Exodus from Egypt, the destruction of Pharoah's army, the fall of the Babylonian Empire and the return of the captives to Jerusalem, the healing and justification of Job, and above all, the Resurrection of the holy, crucified Jesus. Less spectacular signs are evident in the life of every one of us. But this doesn't mean that God's justice reigns in this world. That is why we pray, "Thy Kingdom [the Kingdom of justice] come" and "teach me Thy statutes." If our prayers are sincere we will hasten the establishment of this reign of justice, for God will inspire us to actively seek His liberating justice.[26]

The Book of Daniel is the first to show us that God's justice triumphs only after the resurrection of the dead, i.e., in the Kingdom of God (Dan 12:2).[27] The linking of the belief in retribution beyond the tomb to a belief in the resurrection of the dead appears quite late in the Old Testament, but it is clearly expressed by Christ.

B) God's Judgment in the New Testament

"Do not marvel at this; for the hour is coming when all who are in the tombs will hear His voice and come forth, those who have done good, to the resurrection of life, and those who have done evil, to the resurrection of judgment" (Jn 5:28-29). In the fourth ode of the canon for matins of the Sunday of the Last Judgment we sing, "His judgment is without respect of persons; He is not corrupted by the subtlety of lawyers' pleading or the lies of false witnesses." It is good to know that we will be judged by Christ and not by our next door neighbor or classmate, for we know that He who judges us also loves us. St Paul says, "God shows His love for us in that while we were yet sinners Christ died for us" (Rom 5:8). This Judge spoke through the mouth of His prophet Ezekiel saying, "I have no pleasure in the death of the wicked, but that the wicked turn from his way and live" (Ezek 33:11). St Paul explains further, "[He] desires all men to be saved and to come to the knowledge of the truth" (1 Tim 2:4). Peter also says, "The Lord . . . is forbearing toward you,

26. See p. 52.
27. See chapter 35, p. 356.

not wishing that any should perish, but that all should reach repentance" (2 Pet 3:9). It is good news indeed that we will be judged by Christ.

Seeker: If Christ is our Judge, what laws will He judge us by?

Sage: If Christ were to judge us according to the Law of Moses, in the same way that judges of this world use the penal code, no one would be saved. We would all be condemned, "for no human being will be justified in His sight by works of the law" (Rom 3:20). We all need mercy, so let's be merciful ourselves. "Blessed are the merciful, for they shall obtain mercy" (Mt 5:7). "Be merciful, even as your Father is merciful. Judge not, and you will not be judged; condemn not, and you will not be condemned" (Lk 6:36-37).

Jesus is here speaking not only of our "visible" neighbors, but also of "the least of My brethren," the image of God which is present in each one of us.

C) *The Last Judgment*

Christ describes the Last Judgment in the parable of the sheep and the goats:

> Then the King will say to those at His right hand, "Come, O blessed of My Father, inherit the kingdom prepared for you from the foundation of the world; for I was hungry and you gave Me food, I was thirsty and you gave Me drink, I was a stranger and you welcomed Me, I was naked and you clothed Me, I was sick and you visited Me, I was in prison and you came to Me." (Mt 25:34-36)

Thus our own fate will depend on the way we have treated the suffering,[28] for Christ is hidden in everyone who is sick, in every immigrant, in every prison inmate. We may not recognize Him as we help them, but Christ will recognize *us* on the Day of Judgment and permit us to enter into His Kingdom.

---

28. Isaiah had already said this (Is 58:7): "Shelter the homeless poor," and "clothe the man you see naked."

Then the righteous will answer Him, "Lord, when did we see Thee hungry and feed Thee, or thirsty and give Thee drink? . . ." And the King will answer them, "Truly, I say to you, as you did it to one of the least of these My brethren, you did it to Me." (Mt 25:37,40)

We look for God everywhere and yet He is close by, in the person of His only Son. He is hidden in the little old lady next door and the man down the block who digs ditches, people whom we have never invited to our table. Let us make sure that the King does not say to us, as He will to those on His left hand on that Day,

"Depart from Me, you cursed, into the eternal fire prepared for the devil and his angels;[29] for I was hungry and you gave Me no food, I was thirsty and you gave Me no drink, I was a stranger and you did not welcome Me, naked and you did not clothe Me, sick and in prison and you did not visit Me . . . [For] as you did it not to one of the least of these, you did it not to Me." And they will go away into eternal punishment, but the righteous into eternal life. (Mt 25:41-43, 45-46)

Seeker: If there's eternal punishment, how can you speak of God's love?

Sage: God Himself gives you an answer through the mouth of John the Evangelist: "For God so loved the world that He gave His only Son, that whoever believes in Him should not perish but have eternal life" (Jn 3:16). God ardently desires our salvation from eternal death, even at the price of His Son's life. But God respects our freedom. He does not save us against our will, He does not force us to love Him. St John Chrysostom says "God does not draw anyone to Himself by force or violence. He desires the salvation of all, but does not force anyone." He offers us life at His side, where we shall be "fellow heirs with Christ, provided we suffer with Him in order that we may also be glorified with Him" (Rom 8:17). But we are given the free choice

---

29. Note (see St John Chrysostom, *Homily* 79) that this fire has been prepared not for men, but for the devil and his angels. Nor was it prepared "from the creation of the world": evil is not a part of God's plan for creation.

to reject Him, to turn away from Life and choose death, a death which St John in Revelation calls "the second death," and St Matthew calls "eternal punishment."

And so at every moment of our lives we make the choices by which we shall later be judged, which even at this moment can lead us from death to life and which show that we are "children of God" (1 Jn 3:10). "We know that we have passed out of death into life, because we love the brethren. He who does not love abides in death" (1 Jn 3:14). To go from hatred to love is to pass from death to life and in some way to forestall the Last Judgment. "Heaven on earth is the Eucharist and the love of one's neighbor," St John Chrysostom tells us.

But it's easy to *talk* of loving one's enemies; it's much harder actually to love them; "Little children, let us not love in word or speech but in deed and in truth" (1 Jn 3:18).

Seeker: I find some people irritating and unpleasant. How can I love them if they aggravate me? Won't I be a hypocrite if I pretend to love them?

Sage: To change the taste of a glass of water, you must pour in something that tastes good. If you want to change your heart so that "your heart of stone becomes a heart of flesh," it must be touched by a new presence. St John tells us that "God is love" and "love is of God" (1 Jn 4:16,7). To love our enemies, or simply those whom we dislike, we must accept the love of Him who is Love. We must address ourselves to Him with confidence and faith, for faith leads us to love: "we know and believe the love God has for us" (1 Jn 4:16). "In this the love of God was made manifest among us, that God sent His only Son into the world, so that we might live through Him . . . Whoever confesses that Jesus is the Son of God, God abides in him, and he in God" (1 Jn 4:9,15). It is by believing in Jesus Christ that we discover that God loved us so much, that He gave us His only Son. When we discover that we are loved, we ourselves begin to love: "We love, because He first loved us" (1 Jn 4:19).

Faith leads us to love. The reverse is also true: love leads us to faith, for it is through true love that we discover God. "He who loves is born of God and knows God. He who does not love does not know God; for God is love" (1 Jn 4:7-8).

To believe and to love are one and the same thing. This is God's commandment, that we should cleave to His Son Jesus Christ and love one another. Then we are truly "born of God": "We know that any one born of God does not sin, but He who was born of God [that is, the Son Jesus Christ] keeps him, and the evil one does not touch him" (1 Jn 5:18-19). "He does not come into judgment, but has passed from death to life" (Jn 5:24). Thus we are able to overcome Judgment through love.

CHAPTER 39

PRAYER FOR THE DEAD
AND THE COMMUNION OF THE SAINTS

Salvation is personal. This means that every individual is responsible for his own life before God. It does not mean that fellowship among men, which is pleasing to God, should not exist. At times the Bible emphasizes individual responsibility and at times the solidarity of all.

In the Book of Ezekiel God emphasizes the first:

> When a land sins against Me by acting faithlessly, and I stretch out My hand against it . . . even if these three men, Noah, Daniel and Job, were in it, they would deliver only their own lives by their righteousness, says the Lord God. If I cause wild beasts to pass through the land, and they ravage it, and it be made desolate . . . even if these three men were in it, as I live, says the Lord God, they would deliver neither sons nor daughters; they alone would be delivered, but the land would be desolate. (Ezek 14:13-16)

Thus God saves the righteous even when everyone else is unfaithful, but the unfaithful cannot take advantage of the righteous to gain salvation.

However, in the Book of Genesis (18:23-32), God tells us that He would save a whole city for the sake of ten righteous. He tells Abraham, who is imploring His mercy, "If I find at Sodom fifty righteous in the city, I will spare the whole place for their sake . . . For the sake of ten I will not destroy it." That is why the apostle James says, "Pray for one another . . . The prayer of a righteous man has great power" (Jas 5:16).

That is also why St Steven begged the Lord to be merciful to those who were stoning him (Acts 7:60). He knew that God's mercy is as infinite as His justice, and that the prayer of the righteous can obtain forgiveness for sinners. He followed the example of Christ who prayed for those who were crucifying Him, "Father, forgive them; for they know not what they do" (Lk 23:34).

The prayer of the righteous can also help to obtain forgiveness for a sinner even if he is already dead. In the Second Book of Maccabees[30] we read:

> For if he were not expecting that those who had fallen would rise again, it would have been superfluous and foolish to pray for the dead. But if he was looking to the splendid reward that is laid up for those who fall asleep in godliness, it was a holy and pious thought. Therefore he made atonement for the dead, that they might be delivered from their sin. (2 Mac 12:44-45)

By praying for the dead, we hope to obtain their pardon. And St John reveals in Revelation that the dead can also pray for the living (5:8; 8:3). He even compares the prayer of the saints before the throne of the Lamb to "golden bowls full of incense." Death does not shatter the unity of Christ's body: the members of the Church who are still struggling in this world and those who have already received their reward in the next, are part of the same Body. This is the communion of the saints.[31]

Thus the Divine Liturgy is celebrated by the whole Church: the pilgrim Church of those who are still "in the flesh" and the glorified Church of those who are already "with Christ," "away from the body and at home with the Lord" (Phil 1:22, 23; 2 Cor 5:8). These saints who contemplate the face of God are represented in our churches on the icons which surround the faithful. They are also represented in the Divine Liturgy by the particles (small pieces of bread) which the priest puts on the paten[32] as he reads the names written by the faithful on the diptychs.[33] When the priest prepares the eucharistic

---

30. Maccabees: a) see p. 367, chapter 37, part C; b) the name of this book is taken from its primary personage, Judas Maccabeus.
31. See also Wis 3:7.
32. Paten: see Part VI, p. 287.
33. Diptychs: double sheets of paper on which the faithful inscribe the names of living and dead persons for whom they wish the Church to pray.

offering, he first places on the paten a piece of bread called "the
Lamb" which will become the Body of Christ and will be given to
the faithful as Communion. Then he places a small triangular piece
of bread on the right of the Lamb to commemorate the Theotokos.
On the left of the Lamb he places nine small pieces of bread
representing St John the Baptist, prophets, apostles, holy hierarchs
(bishops), martyrs, ascetics,[34] unmercenary healers, the ancestors of
Christ, and the saint whose liturgy is being celebrated (St. John
Chrysostom or St. Basil the Great). Then at the foot of the Lamb
he places particles representing the living, and below them particles
representing the dead whose names were written on the diptychs.
Thus the whole Church, united around its Head, is represented on
the paten.[35] During the anaphora it will be offered to God, and He
sanctifies it by His Holy Spirit.[36]

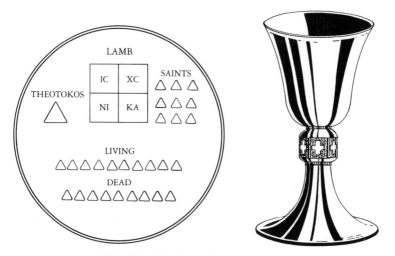

The Distribution of Bread on the Paten

34. Ascetics: those who have practiced ascesis, i.e., who have submitted their bodies and
    souls to strict discipline in order to place them under the exclusive control of the Lord.
35. See the illustration above: the arrangement of the bread on the paten.
36. See Part VI, chapter 24, p. 292: "The Anaphora."

A) *The Communion of the Saints*

Seeker: You're telling me about saints on the paten, but what is a saint?

Sage: When the priest says, "The Holy things for the holy," the people answer, "One is Holy. One is Lord Jesus Christ, to the glory of God the Father. Amen."

Seeker: How can men be called holy when only the Lord Jesus Christ is holy?

Sage: Those whom we call holy became holy only by acquiring the Holy Spirit and participating in the life of the only Holy One, who said, "You, therefore, must be perfect, as your heavenly Father is perfect" (Mt 5:48).

Seeker: Are they virtuous then?

Sage: They are, but that's not the most essential. A saint is someone who does the will of God (cf. Jn 7:16-18; also Jn 5:30).

Seeker: How can we do His will?

Sage: St Paul says, "I do not do what I want, but I do the very thing I hate" (Rom 7:15). This is part of the human condition. We follow our impulses, we pursue our personal interests, the interests of the "old man." But in the Epistle to the Galatians (2:20) he says, ". . . it no longer I who live, but Christ who lives in me." Now Paul is able to do the Father's will, for "our old self was crucified with Him [i.e., Christ] so that the sinful body might be destroyed, and we might no longer be enslaved to sin. For he who has died is freed from sin . . . Let not sin therefore reign in your mortal bodies, to make you obey their passions" (Rom 6:6-7, 12).

Seeker: Then I must try to become better?

Sage: Yes, but that's not enough. You can do nothing on your own except become proud, for "apart from Me you can do nothing" (Jn 15:5). You attain Life only by following the Master, by taking up your cross, by letting the dead bury their dead (Mt 8:22 and Lk 9:60).

Seeker: Why did Jesus say, "Let the dead bury their dead?" It bothers me.

Sage: Indeed, it is disturbing. The dead (and living) of whom Christ speaks are those who do not seek the Life of the Kingdom. What

Jesus in fact says is: "Leave the dead to bury their own dead; but as for you, go and proclaim the Kingdom of God" (Lk 9:60). For the living, for those who have set out on the path of holiness and who seek Christ, the only Living One, the cares of this world seem unimportant compared to the Life of the Kingdom.

Seeker: What happens to these "dead"? Is there any hope for them?

Sage: If they have "ears to hear" (Mt 11:15) and are attentive to the Holy Spirit they will be able to hear the Lord say, "Follow Me" (Mt 8:22); and they will rejoin the living members of His flock.

Seeker: And what if they don't listen to the Word and don't rejoin the flock?

Sage: Then they will end up like the wicked servant who buried his talent (Mt 25:24-30), for "No one who puts his hand to the plow and looks back is fit for the kingdom of God" (Lk 9:62).

Seeker: But isn't hearing the Word and following it what is called a "vocation"?

Sage: Yes, that is also true. Whoever hears the voice of the Master enters upon the narrow path which leads to Life. He lives through his own judgment, as St Seraphim of Sarov did during the twenty-five years of his life as a recluse. Even during his life on earth such a person overflows with the Holy Spirit; he has already been resurrected. His earthly death will be simply a passage towards greater fullness. He will enter into the joy of his Master. He will fall into the arms of the Father like the prodigal son and will never again leave him. As St Paul says, "so we shall always be with the Lord" (1 Thess 4:17).

Saints are those who perpetuate the Church's Pentecost, those who are living witnesses of the presence of the Holy Spirit. That is why the Orthodox Church celebrates their feast on the Sunday after Pentecost, the Sunday of All Saints.[37]

Seeker: Why does the Mother of God have a special place on the paten?

---

37. The Roman Catholics celebrate All-Saints on November 1, the eve of the "Feast of the Dead."

Sage: The Theotokos has a special place at the right hand of Christ because she gives us the most perfect example of the passage from death to life. The dormition of the Theotokos is the best example of a perfect end to our earthly existence, for she passed into eternal life without going through the Judgment. As the Gospel says: "Truly, truly, I say to you, he who hears My word and believes Him who sent Me, has eternal life; he does not come into judgment, but has passed from death to life" (Jn 5:24).

CHAPTER 40

THE FALLING ASLEEP OF THE MOST HOLY THEOTOKOS

Holy Scripture does not tell us about the dormition of the Theotokos,[38] but the story has been preserved in the memory of the Church. We get a glimpse of this mystery in the icon of the feast and the Liturgy of August 15.

A) The Icon of the Falling Asleep of the Most Holy Theotokos

Mary is lying on her deathbed. The Holy Spirit has brought the apostles together from all corners of the world to be with her at her death. She is also surrounded by the first bishops of the Church. The angels bow before her and women come to venerate her body. Jesus, luminous in glory, stands at the center behind the deathbed, holding a child in His arms. This child represents His mother's soul.

Seeker: Why does the soul look like a child? Is it a miniature body which houses the soul?

Sage: No, Mary is given the form of a newborn baby in swaddling clothes because she is born anew in heaven. She brought the Son of God into this world in the flesh, she endowed him with humanity so that He might be born on earth. And this Son now endows her with His divinity so that she may be reborn in heaven. "The glory of the age to come, the final end of man, is already realized, not only in a divine Hypostasis made flesh, but also in a human person made God."[39]

---

38. This feast is called Assumption by the Roman Catholics.
39. V. Lossky, in Ouspensky and Lossky, *The Meaning of Icons* (Berne: Urs Graf Verlag, 1952, 2nd edition), p. 215.

The Dormition of the Theotokos

Troparion of Dormition

Common Chant
arr. from LVOV-BAKHMETEV

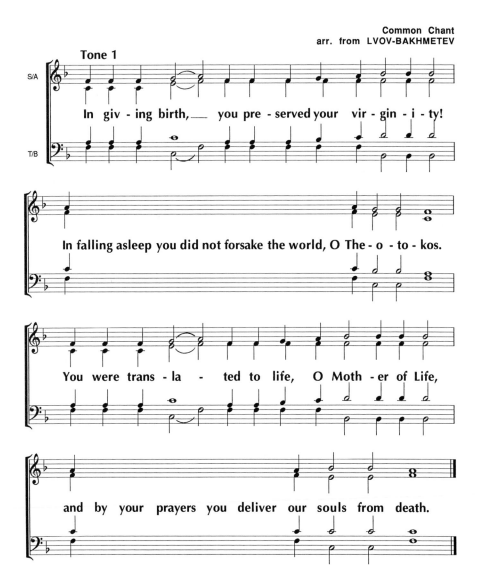

Tone 1

In giv - ing birth, ___ you pre - served your vir - gin - i - ty!

In falling asleep you did not forsake the world, O The - o - to - kos.

You were trans - la - ted to life, O Moth - er of Life,

and by your prayers you deliver our souls from death.

B) *The Liturgy of August 15*

In the troparion of the Dormition we sing:

In giving birth, you preserved your virginity!
In falling asleep you did not forsake the world, O Theotokos!
You were translated to life, O Mother of Life,
And by your prayers you deliver our souls from death!
(tone 1)

The Dormition service teaches us that Mary passed from death to life and that she entered into eternal life without going through Judgment (Jn 5:24), for the Mother of Life could not be overcome by corruption. On August 15 we celebrate a second Pascha, the resurrection of her who is already united to Christ before the Last Judgment and the general resurrection.

Neither the tomb, nor death, could hold the Theotokos,
Who is constant in prayer and our firm hope in her intercessions.
For being the Mother of Life,
She was translated to life by the One who dwelt in her
    virginal womb!
(Kontakion of the feast, tone 2)

The angels beheld the dormition of the Pure One and were amazed.
How has the Virgin gone up from earth to heaven?
(Megalynarion of the second canon for matins, tone 4)

A verse from vespers tells us that the apostles witnessed a second Ascension: that of Mary in her body, so that she might share the glory of her Son.

What has already been accomplished with Mary is part of God's plan for each one of us. At the end of time, after the Last Judgment, we shall live before the face of God in the fullness of body and soul. St Paul exclaims:

What is sown is perishable, what is raised is imperishable. It is sown in dishonor, it is raised in glory. It is sown in weakness, it is raised in power. It is sown a physical body, it is raised a spiritual body. (1 Cor 15:42-44)

Thus through the Judgment we are led into eternal life in the heavenly Jerusalem.

CHAPTER 41

THE HEAVENLY JERUSALEM

Seeker: We've talked about the Lord's First Coming, about the meaning of the Incarnation, and about the period of the Church, that is, our own time, a time of struggle. Now we wait for the Second Coming, "the resurrection of the dead, and the life of the world to come" (the Creed).

I'm really impressed by what you've told me, especially about the end of the world. You say that the destruction of the old world is a necessary prelude to the creation of the new. But I recently heard a lecture by an astrophysicist, a famous astronomer. He predicted "the tragic end of our sun," saying that one day the sun will explode and burn up the earth. This will be the end of mankind. Such an end is very realistically portrayed in many books and films. You, on the other hand, describe the end as a transition into God's eternal love, as eternal life in a heavenly Jerusalem. Is the end of which you speak completely different from the one described by the physicist?

Sage: They are not on the same plane. Science functions within the limits of this world. It deals only with an empirical and rational reality. But revelation goes far beyond the temporal limits within which scientific research is confined.

We have a different way of looking at things, although we do not ignore science any more than we try to free ourselves from history. We know that the Lord is the "Alpha and the Omega" (Rev 1:8), the Principle, the Creator, the Center, and the End of everything, "for from Him and through Him and to Him are all things" (Rom 11:36). We can discover this by entering into the mystery of the Scriptures.

We cannot do this on our own, and so at every Liturgy, before the reading of the Scriptures, we ask God, "Illumine our hearts, O

Master who lovest mankind, with the pure light of Thy divine knowledge. Open the eyes of our mind to the understanding of Thy gospel teachings." Let us now turn to the heavenly Jerusalem which has been promised to us.

During our conversations and my explanations we constantly came across the words "covenant" and "promise." One must never forget these words, for God is faithful and the offer of His covenant is always open to us. In the Scriptures this is expressed through many forms, images, and symbols: the Kingdom of God, the Reign, the salvation of Israel, the Lord's Coming, the wedding banquet of the Lamb and His people, the betrothal of the Church and her Lord, the earth, the Temple, the dwelling, the City of God, Zion, the life of the world to come, the new Jerusalem, the heavenly Jerusalem. What God promises is a radically new world.

But be careful. The coming of this new world is an eternal and dynamic truth which is expressed simultaneously on two levels, that of human history and that of divine mystery. This Kingdom is present both here and now and "is to come"; it is eternal and yet absolutely new. This newness is closely connected with the ultimate vocation of all living creatures which is to freely attain union with God. Theologians call this "deification" (*theosis*). Furthermore, "This is the positive definition of the same mystery, which must be accomplished in each human person in the Church and which will be fully revealed in the age to come, when, after having reunited all things in Christ, God will become all in all."[40] As you can see, "vocation" and "future age" are closely linked.

Seeker: Then the end of the world does not mean the end of everything?

Sage: Certainly not. "For the form of this world is passing away" (1 Cor 7:31). "The last enemy to be destroyed is death" (1 Cor 15:26). "The Church is the image and sign of the kingdom of God because the kingdom begins as a seed and as leaven in today's Church . . ."[41]

---

40. Vladimir Lossky, *In the Image and Likeness of God,* (Crestwood, NY: St. Vladimir's Seminary Press), 1974, p. 110.
41. Ignatius Hazim.

"But though creation is contingent in its origin and began to exist, it will never cease to be; death and destruction will not involve a return to non-being, for 'the word of the Lord endures for ever' (I Pet 1:25), and the divine will is unchangeable."[42]

These promises, which are full of hope for us, can be found throughout the Scriptures.

A) In the Old Testament

Throughout the Old Testament we come across the image of a radically new world: "Behold, I am doing a new thing; now it springs forth, do you not perceive it?" (Is 43:19).

We hear a cry of hope in the promise which is echoed from text to text. We find the theme of a faithless and chastised Jerusalem which will repent in the end, be created anew and accepted back as "a Bride" (Is 62:5) in whom God will rejoice.

Most of the positive words found in the Old Testament are used to describe the heavenly Jerusalem. These descriptive expressions help us to understand the mystery. To the terms we have already mentioned we should add the Light (Is 60:1, 3; Ps 35:10 [36:9]), the Face, and God's Strength.

The text which is most expressive of this hope is Isaiah 65:17-25:

> For behold, I create new heaven and a new earth; and the former things shall not be remembered or come into mind. But be glad and rejoice for ever in that which I create; for behold, I create Jerusalem a rejoicing, and her people a joy. I will rejoice in Jerusalem, and be glad in My people; no more shall be heard in it the sound of weeping and the cry of distress. No more shall there be in it an infant that lives but a few days, or an old man who does not fill out his days, . . . They shall be the offspring of the blessed of the Lord, and their children with them. Before they call I will answer, while they are yet speaking I will hear. The wolf

---

42. Vladimir Lossky, *The Mystical Theology of the Eastern Church.*

and the lamb shall feed together, the lion shall eat straw like the ox; the dust shall be the serpent's food. They shall not hurt or destroy in all My holy mountain, says the Lord. (Is 65:17-20, 23-25)

Jerusalem or Zion, the city of peace (Ps 75:3, LXX), is a personification of the chosen people. "And they shall be called the holy people . . ." (Is 62:12). It is the dwelling place of God (Ps 2:6; 109 [110]:2; 134 [135]:21); "and all the nations shall flow to it" (Is 2:2). At the time of Moses God had dwelt in a tent, but the new Jerusalem will be the dwelling place of the Lord forever (Ps 75:3 [76:2]; 86 [87]:2; 106 [107]:3; 131 [132]:13-14; 134 [135]:21).

It is true that it is sometimes difficult to tell whether the text refers to the earthly or the heavenly Jerusalem. But we know that the earthly Jerusalem is only a shadow of the heavenly one, which will appear at the end of time. It will be built of "living stones" (1 Pet 2:5), that is, of the people who are its citizens. We must always remember this spiritual homeland. "If I forget you, O Jerusalem, let my right hand wither!" (Ps 136 [137]:5).

Seeker: But how could a city built of stone be called "the city of our God" (Ps 47:9 [48:8]); how could one say of it, "This one and that one were born in her" (Ps 86 [87]:5)?

Sage: In the psalms David describes the divine character of "the city of David" (2 Sam 5:9) many times: "Thou, O God, art my fortress" (Ps 58:10 [59:9]); ". . . the city of our God! His holy mountain, beautiful in elevation, is the joy of all the earth" (Ps 47:2-3 [48:1-2]).

The Lord makes "an everlasting covenant" with Israel, the chosen people, personified by Jerusalem. It is here that He establishes His sanctuary forever (Ezek 37:26). He will wash the people of all their sins and will give them "a new heart." "A new Spirit I will put within you; and I will take out of your flesh the heart of stone and give you a heart of flesh" (Ezek 36:26). This promise still lives in the hearts of men and women, and it is still upon this covenant that everything depends. The Lord says to Israel as to His betrothed: "And I will betroth you to Me for ever; I will betroth you to Me in righteousness and in justice, in steadfast love and in mercy . . . I will

say . . . 'You are My people'; and you shall say, 'Thou art my God'"
(Hos 2:19, 23). He will overwhelm His betrothed with "the goodness
of [His] house, [His] holy temple!" (Ps 64:5 [65:4]). Then there will
be great joy, for the city will praise God. "Blessed are those who dwell
in Thy house, ever singing Thy praise!" (Ps 83:5 [84:4]).

Eusebius, a fourth century writer, explains that the foundations
of the celestial Jerusalem are high up on the holy mountain, but its
gates are here below. They are the gates of the Church, which are
the gates of the heavenly Kingdom. Thus we are reminded that the
way to our true homeland, the heavenly Jerusalem, is through the
Church.

B) *In the New Testament*

The Beatitudes renew these ancient promises. This time it is our
Lord Jesus Christ Himself who speaks: "Blessed are the poor in spirit,
for theirs is the kingdom of heaven. Blessed are those who mourn,
for they shall be comforted . . . Blessed are those who are persecuted
for righteousness' sake, for theirs is the kingdom of heaven" (Mt
5:34, 10). In another part of the same Gospel we read: "Let the
children come to Me, and do not hinder them; for to such belongs
the kingdom of heaven" (Mt 19:14). "Then the righteous will shine
like the sun in the kingdom of their Father" (Mt 13:43).

The parable of the wedding feast (Mt 22:1-14) compares the
Kingdom of God to a wedding feast where those who wear "the
wedding garment," those who thirst for light, God, and the Holy
Spirit, participate in the wedding feast of the king's son. This does
not simply mean that we must observe certain rites and rules. Rather,
we must be born anew of water and the Spirit (Jn 3:1-21), to be born
into a new life. Jesus' conversation with Nicodemus emphasizes this
paradoxical need to be reborn in order to enter into the Kingdom
(Jn 3:3).

St Paul repeats this same idea: "If anyone is in Christ, he is a new
creation" (2 Cor 5:17).

Writing to the Galatians he also speaks of the heavenly Jerusalem.
He reminds them that Abraham had two sons, one from a slave and

the other from a free woman. And he continues: ". . . these women are two covenants. One is from Mount Sinai, bearing children for slavery; . . . she corresponds to the present Jerusalem, for she is in slavery with her children. But the Jerusalem above is free, and she is our mother" (Gal 4:24-26).

The Epistle to the Hebrews evokes the same thought: "But you have come to Mount Zion and to the city of the living God, the heavenly Jerusalem" (Heb 12:22).

St Peter speaks of the Day of the Lord, affirming that "according to His promise we wait for new heavens and a new earth in which righteousness dwells" (2 Pet 3:13).

Finally we come to the last book of the Bible, the Apocalypse, which means "revelation." John calls it the revelation of Jesus Christ. It is a mysterious text full of enigmas and symbols, a last prophecy, the culmination of all the aspirations of the people of the Old Testament enlightened by the revelation of Jesus Christ. The last two chapters of this book deal with the heavenly Jerusalem and the new creation. The first, old creation had been described in the first two chapters of the Bible. After the tumults of wars and scourges, after the description of prophetic and enigmatic events, we sense a change in John's tone. We get the impression that "with fear and trembling" we are approaching the Kingdom, a blissful eternity flooded with divine Light.

> Then I saw a new heaven and a new earth; for the first heaven and the first earth had passed away, and the sea was no more. And I saw the holy city, new Jerusalem, coming down out of heaven from God, prepared as a bride adorned for her husband. And I heard a loud voice from the throne saying, "Behold, the dwelling of God is with men. He will dwell with them, and they shall be His people, and God Himself will be with them. He will wipe away every tear from their eyes, and death shall be no more, neither shall there be mourning nor crying nor pain any more, for the former things have passed away." And He who sat upon the throne said, "Behold, I make all things new . . . I am the Alpha and the Omega, the beginning and the end. To the thirsty I will give from the fountain of the water of life without payment. He who conquers shall have

this heritage, and I will be his God and he shall be My son." (Rev 21:1-7)

Then came one of the seven angels . . . and spoke to me, saying, "Come, I will show you the Bride, the wife of the Lamb." And . . . [he] showed me the holy city Jerusalem coming down out of heaven from God, having the glory of God. (Rev 21:9-11)

There shall no more be anything accursed, but the throne of God and of the Lamb shall be in it, and His servants shall worship Him; they shall see His face, and His name shall be on their foreheads. (Rev 22:3-4)

Notice the words, "they shall see His face." The Kingdom is the presence of God.

The main theme of Revelation is the glorious coming of the Lord who will reign "for ever and ever" (Rev 22:5) with the people of God in a new and heavenly Jerusalem where truth will be communion and life. But there remains a mystery: "No eye has seen, nor ear heard, nor the heart of man conceived, what God has prepared for those who love Him" (1 Cor 2:9; Is 64:4).

Seeker: When we recite the Lord's prayer and say, "Thy Kingdom come," are we also referring to this Kingdom?

Sage: Yes, it is the same word (*basileia* in Greek) translated in two different ways. There is a deep and mysterious connection between the Kingdom which germinates and grows in our hearts and the Kingdom for which we are waiting and which is coming.

C) In Liturgical Texts

During the Liturgy of St John Chrysostom, the priest concludes one of his prayers with the words: "Grant them to worship Thee blamelessly with fear and love, . . . and to be accounted worthy of Thy heavenly Kingdom."

During the anaphora he says: "Thou it was who brought us from nonexistence into being, . . . and didst not cease to do all things until Thou hadst brought us up to heaven, and hadst endowed us with Thy Kingdom which is to come."

After the consecration of the Gifts, the priest asks that "they may be to those who partake . . . for the fulfillment of the Kingdom of Heaven."

After Communion the deacon says: "O Wisdom, Word and Power of God! Grant that we may more perfectly partake of Thee in the never-ending Day of Thy Kingdom."

During the Sacrament of Chrismation, which follows immediately after Baptism, the priest prays: "Confirm him in the Orthodox faith; . . . that he . . . may become a child and heir of Thy heavenly Kingdom."

During matins of Holy Thursday the choir sings: "Thou didst say to Thy friends, O Christ: 'In my Kingdom I shall drink a new vintage beyond understanding, so that I shall be with you as God among gods. For the Father has sent me, the only-begotten Son, into the world as its atonement'" (fourth ode).

During matins on Easter night, the "feast of feasts, holy day of holy days," we sing a triumphant irmos which is repeated as the hymn to the Theotokos at both the Paschal Liturgy and all the Liturgies during the paschal season. It is also said by the deacon after Communion at every Liturgy throughout the year: "Shine! Shine! O New Jerusalem! The glory of the Lord has shone on you! Exult now and be glad, O Zion!"

Later in the paschal matins we also sing: "Come from that scene, O women, bearers of glad tidings, and say to Zion: 'Receive from us the glad tidings of joy, of Christ's resurrection. Exult and be glad, and rejoice, O Jerusalem, seeing Christ the King, who comes forth from the tomb like a bridegroom in procession.'" One must hear these chants in order to understand the joy which fills the hearts of the faithful when the risen Christ comes forth from the tomb and the Kingdom of God is already with us.

Seeker: I have felt this joy and I would like to keep it through the rest of the year.

Sage: At the beginning of Revelation we read that the Lord is He "who is and who was and who is to come" (Rev 1:8). His presence is always the source of life for us. John says: "The Spirit and the

Bride say 'Come.' And let him who hears say, 'Come.' And let him who is thirsty come, let him who desires take the water of life without price" (Rev 22:17).

Listen also to the last words of the Bible: "He who testifies to these things says, 'Surely I am coming soon.' Amen. Come, Lord Jesus!" (Rev 22:20).

Appendix—Initiation in Prayer

Table of Contents

A. Prologue
B. Selected daily prayers traditionally used by Orthodox Christians

Initiation to Prayer

A) Prologue

God and man are not machines. Both are free persons; this is why there are no ready-made formulas which enable us automatically to enter into a relationship with God. It is God Himself who has taken the initiative in our encounter with Him. It is He who has come to us by sending to us His Son and the Holy Spirit, the Spirit who enables us to know God and who teaches us to pray to Him. The word that we hear when the Lord speaks to us in the Gospel, and the breath which fills our heart when the Spirit touches it, are the teachers who teach us how to pray. It is they who, by the mouth of Jesus Himself, or by the mouth of His servant, are the true authors of the several prayers that we are going to quote. May these prayers serve to move our own lips and the heart of the reader, enabling him to raise his voice towards the Father, through the inspiration of the Holy Spirit, so that his whole being enters into harmonious praise with the voice of the universal Church.

First of all we must understand that prayer is profoundly rooted in the Word of God. In order to do so, let us read once again the text in Genesis chapter 32, which describes Jacob's struggle with God. After their struggle, God blessed Jacob because "he had been strong against God," strong in the presence of God. In some sense, God wanted to make Himself vulnerable to man. By their struggle, God and man joined together in a particular way; there is a movement in this dialogue from divinity itself towards man. Here we discover the movement of God towards man and the return of man towards God. The Church, in fact, calls each of us to assume this movement of return to God. For it is precisely this movement that creates the essential framework of both individual and liturgical prayer.

There is no opposition between liturgical and personal prayer, for even when a Christian prays in isolation, he is never alone. Christ accompanies him in and through his prayer. And through the presence of Christ, the one who prays is accompanied as well by the whole

community of the Church, with which he receives communion in the
very Body of Christ.

B) A Selection of Daily Prayers traditionally used by Orthodox Christians

Morning Prayers

1) Invocation to the Holy Spirit

> O Heavenly King, the Comforter, the Spirit of Truth, who art
> everywhere present and fillest all things. Treasury of blessings and
> giver of life, come and abide in us; cleanse us from every impurity,
> and save our souls, O Good One.

This prayer was composed by the Fathers of the Church during
the first Christian centuries (ca. third or fourth century). It is also
one of the hymns sung at the vigil service of Pentecost. The service
of Pentecost offers us an exceptionally rich and full teaching on the
theology of the Holy Trinity. There is no theology more living or
more full of life than the one offered to us by the services of the
great feasts. For it is in them that we receive the fullest possible
teaching mediated by divine Beauty. This Beauty is reflected in the
ancient poems created by the first Christian communities in the
hymns whose words harmonize so well with sacred music, and
especially in the Church itself gathered together in celebration in
order to offer up its prayer to God.

Pentecost is both the fulfillment and the beginning of all things.
It is first of all the fulfillment of the divine plan within the history
of salvation. Jesus has come and has accomplished all things even
unto death, including His resurrection and His ascension to the
Father. As we wait for His second coming, He sends to us from the
Father the gift of the Holy Spirit, the Paraclete, the Spirit of Truth
(John 14:16-17).

The Holy Spirit who descended upon the apostles is truly the
fulfillment, the very crowning of the life of Jesus upon the earth.
Now God dwells within the entire universe, for "the spirit of truth

is everywhere present and fills all things." "It is better for you that I depart; for if I do not leave you the Paraclete will not come to you, (and it is He who) will lead you into all the truth" (John 16:7-17). These are the words which Jesus spoke on that night in the upper room, and which St John relates to us in his Gospel.

The coming of the Holy Spirit upon the apostles is the fulfillment of the total self-revelation of the Holy Trinity; and it is also the beginning, for all things begin on that day of Pentecost. The life of the Church surges forth from the very fire of Pentecost. On that day everything begins anew in such a way as to have no end, even into eternity: "Behold, I make all things new," Jesus declares (Revelation 21:5).

In a definite sense, the last times have already been inaugurated with Pentecost. The Holy Spirit is the life of the Church; in Him the presence of God continues upon earth until the second and final coming of our Lord. Our life within the Church is a continual outreach towards the Kingdom which is to come. That is why this prayer so specific to the feast of Pentecost, the "O heavenly King," is prayed throughout the whole of the liturgical year.[1]

Without Pentecost and the gift of the Holy Spirit, the Giver of Life, the Church would be nothing other than a dead letter; it would know nothing other than an everlasting recycling of liturgical ritual. With the Holy Spirit, however, all things take on a new life. From this moment on, liturgical time means no longer monotonous or automatic repetition day after day. It becomes a creative tension, forever renewed even into eternity.

Now we can understand why every celebration within the Church and every celebration with Christian life, begins with this particular prayer. We recite or we sing "O heavenly King" to begin the day in our morning prayer, before we fall asleep at night during the

---

1. Note only that there is one single exception made during the liturgical year; we do not sing the "O heavenly King" in the paschal season when we live in the presence of the risen Christ with such intensity that everything is replaced by the paschal troparion which proclaims the Resurrection. During the ten days which separate Ascension from Pentecost, we still do not sing "O heavenly King," because we are like the apostles in the Upper Room, waiting in silence for the fulfillment of the Father's promise, that we might be clothed with power from on high (Luke 24:49).

evening prayer, to begin a meeting or gathering of any sort, before any particular undertaking, in the course of catechetical instruction, as well as to begin any ecclesial celebration or service within the Church (vespers, matins, compline, the prayer of the hours). In particular, the Holy Liturgy—which is the most important celebration of our whole life—begins with this invocation to the Holy Spirit. The priest at the altar begins the service, with his hands raised, by quoting "O heavenly King," even before he pronounces the words of the opening benediction: "Blessed is the Kingdom of the Father and of the Son and of the Holy Spirit"—words that actualize from this moment on the reality of the Kingdom to come.

"No one can say Jesus is Lord except by the power of the Holy Spirit" (1 Cor 12:3). In the same way, no one can say "Abba, Father" without the Holy Spirit, "for the Spirit Himself joins with our spirit to testify that we are children of God" (Rom 8:16). We can only draw near to the mystery of God in Trinity through the action of the Holy Spirit within us. No prayer can have life or meaning within us, without the power of the Holy Spirit. That is why we ceaselessly invoke Him.

2) Trisagion

> Holy God! Holy Mighty! Holy Immortal! Have mercy on us. (3 times)
>
> Glory to the Father, and to the Son and to the Holy Spirit, now and ever and unto ages of ages. Amen.
>
> O Most Holy Trinity, have mercy on us! Lord, cleanse us from our sins! Master, pardon our transgressions! Holy One, visit and heal our infirmities for Thy name's sake.
>
> Lord, have mercy! (3 times)
>
> Glory to the Father, and to the Son, and to the Holy Spirit, now and ever and unto ages of ages. Amen

The trinitarian prayer finds its origins in the hymn of the angels heard by the prophet Isaiah in the first year of King Aziah (740 B.C.; Isaiah 6:3); "Holy, holy, holy is the Lord Sabaoth!" Once again—more than seven centuries later—the same cry of praise was heard by the apostle John at the moment of the revelation which he received on the island of Patmos (Revelation 4:8).

This prayer, called the "Trisagion," is commented upon during the vespers of Pentecost by the so called *doxastikon* of the *aposticha:*

> Come people, let us adore the divinity in three persons: the Son in the Father with the Holy Spirit. For outside of time, the Father bore the eternal Son with Him upon the same throne. And the Holy Spirit, glorified with the Son, was in the Father as a unique power, a unique being, a unique divinity, whom we all adore and to whom we say: Holy God, who created the universe by the Son and the cooperation of the Holy Spirit; Holy Mighty, by whom we have come to know the Father and by whom the Holy Spirit has entered into the world; Holy Immortal, Spirit—Paraclete who proceeds from the Father and rests upon the Son; O Holy Trinity, Glory to Thee!

"Holy God" refers particularly to the Father; "Holy Mighty" refers especially to the Son (the expression "Holy Mighty" is taken from Isaiah 9:5, where it referred to "a child born to us, a son given to us"); "Holy Immortal" refers particularly to the Holy Spirit, whom the Nicene Creed qualifies as Creator or Source of life.

In addition, this trinitarian prayer is repeated three times: once for the Father, once for the Son, and once for the Holy Spirit. In fact, we can only address the Father insofar as we think of the Son whom He engenders and the Holy Spirit who proceeds from Him. Similarly, we can only address the Son insofar as we think of the Father who engenders Him, and the Spirit who rests upon Him. And we can only address the Holy Spirit insofar as we think of the Father from whom He proceeds, and of the Son on whom He rests.

Each divine Person is distinct, but there is an eternal "exchange" of each one with the other two. After having asked for mercy, we offer up praise and glory to each of the three Persons: glory to the Father, to the Son, and to the Holy Spirit. Then we address our prayer to the three Persons at once: "O Holy Trinity, have mercy upon us." Note that we use here the singular: for there is only one God.

Then once again we speak to each one of the three Persons separately by saying to the Father: "O Lord wash away our sins" (here we understand: expiation by the redemptive work of the Son). Then we say to the Son: "Master, pardon our iniquities," for "the Son of Man has the power to forgive sins," (Luke 5:24; Matthew 9:6; Mark 2:10). Then we say to the Holy Spirit: "O Holy One, visit and heal our infirmities for Thy name's sake," (for He is the Comforter who communicates to us all the gifts of the Son, John 14:16, 26; 15:26; 16:7, 14).

Then from each of the three we ask mercy, and we call each of them Lord, for the three are God. Finally, we offer praise to them again before reciting the Lord's Prayer.

The Trisagion, then, is the supreme prayer which introduces us into the divine mystery of trinitarian life. It is the most characteristic prayer offered up by Orthodox Christians, and the first one that little children learn, at the same time that they learn to make the sign of the cross with their three fingers joined together: three Persons, one single God.

3) The Lord's Prayer

Our Father, Who art in heaven, hallowed be Thy Name. Thy Kingdom come. Thy will be done, on earth as it is in heaven. Give us this day our daily bread; and forgive us our trespasses, as we forgive those who trespass against us; and lead us not into temptation, but deliver us from evil.

4) Morning Prayer

Having arisen from sleep, we fall down before Thee, O Blessed One, and sing to Thee, O Mighty One, the angelic hymn: Holy! Holy! Holy! art Thou, O God; through the Theotokos, have mercy on us.

Glory to the Father, and to the Son, and to the Holy Spirit.

Having raised me from my bed and from sleep, O Lord, enlighten my mind and heart, and open my lips that I may praise Thee, O Holy Trinity: Holy! Holy! Holy! art Thou, O God; through the Theotokos, have mercy on us.

Now and ever and unto ages of ages. Amen.

The Judge will come suddenly and the acts of every man will be revealed; but in the middle of the night we cry with fear: Holy!

Holy! Holy! art Thou, O God; through the Theotokos, have mercy on us.

Lord, have mercy! (12 times)

5) Hymn to the Holy Virgin

Rejoice, O virgin Theotokos! Mary, full of grace, the Lord is with you. Blessed are you among women, and blessed is the fruit of your womb. For you have borne the Savior of our souls.

6) Prayer of the third hour (9 A.M.)

O Lord, who at the Third Hour didst send down upon thine Apostles thy Holy Spirit: Take not the same from us, O Good One, but renew Him in us who make our supplications unto thee.

Make me a clean heart, O God, and renew a right spirit within me.

O Lord, who at the Third Hour . . .

Cast me not away from thy presence, and take not thy Holy Spirit from me.

O Lord, who at the Third Hour . . . .

7) Prayer of the sixth hour (Noon)

O thou who, on the sixth day and Hour didst nail to the Cross the sin which Adam, through presumption, committed in Paradise: Tear asunder also the handwriting of our iniquities, O Christ God, and save us.

Hear my prayer, O God, and hide not thyself from my petition.

O thou who, on the sixth day and Hour . . .

As for me, I will call upon God, and the Lord shall save me.

O thou who, on the sixth day and Hour . . .

8) Prayer of the ninth hour (3 P.M.)

O thou who, at the Ninth Hour, for our sake didst taste of death in the flesh: Mortify thou the presumption of our flesh, and save us, O Christ God.

Let my complaint come before thee, O Lord: give me understanding, according to thy word.

O thou who, at the Ninth Hour . . .

Let my supplication come before thee, O Lord: deliver me according to thy word.

O thou who, at the Ninth Hour . . .

9) *Prayer at sunset (vesperal hymn)*

O gladsome light of the holy glory of the immortal Father, heavenly, holy, blessed Jesus Christ. Now that we have come to the setting of the sun, and behold the light of evening, we praise God, Father, Son, and Holy Spirit.

For meet it is at all times to worship thee with voices of praise, O Son of God and giver of life: Therefore all the world doth glorify thee.

10) *Evening Prayers at bedtime*

Now that the day has come to a close, I thank thee, O Lord, and entreat that the evening with the night may be guileless; grant this to me, O Saviour, and save me.

Glory to the Father, and to the Son, and to the Holy Spirit.

Now that the day hath passed, I glorify thee, O Master, and entreat that the evening with the night may be without offense; grant this to me, O Saviour, and save me.

Now and ever and unto ages of ages. Amen.

Now that the day hath run its course, I praise thee, O Holy One, and entreat that the evening with the night may be undisturbed; grant this to me, O Saviour, and save me.

Lord, have mercy! (12 times)

11) *Prayer before meals*

The eyes of all wait upon thee, O Lord, and thou givest them their meat in due season; thou openest thy hand and fillest all things living with bounties.

12) *Prayer after meals*

We give thanks to thee, O Christ our God, for Thou hast satisfied us with Thy earthly blessings. Deprive us not of Thy heavenly Kingdom. But, as Thou didst come to Thy disciples and didst grant them peace, so come to us and save us, O Savior.

13) *During Lent: Prayer of St Ephrem of Syria*[2]

O Lord and Master of my life,
take from me the spirit of sloth, faint-heartedness,
lust of power, and idle talk.
But give rather the spirit of chastity,
humility, patience and love to thy servant.
Yea, O Lord and King,
grant me to see my own errors and not to judge my brother,
for Thou art blessed from all ages to all ages. Amen.

This prayer is recited every day by Orthodox faithful during the period of Lent, and it is read twice at the end of each service from Monday through Friday during the same period. We say this prayer a first time, making a prostration after each request. Then we make a semi-prostration (bending over at the waist to touch the floor with outstretched fingers, then standing up straight again); this we do twelve times, saying within ourselves: "O God, cleanse me, a sinner." Finally, we repeat the whole prayer with one final prostration at the very end.

In his book *Great Lent,* Father Alexander Schmemann analyzed this prayer of St Ephrem in a very helpful way. First of all he examined its four negative points:

2. LENT: The lenten period is a period of 40 days which precedes Holy Week. It is consecrated to the preparation of the celebration of our Lord's Passion and Resurrection (just as the lenten period called Advent prepares us for the coming of Christ at the moment of His Nativity). The flood lasted 40 days; Moses remained 40 days upon Mt Sinai before giving the Law of God to the people; Israel spent 40 years in the desert before entering into the promised land; Elijah walked 40 days and 40 nights before encountering the Lord at Mt Horeb; the Lord Jesus fasted for 40 days in the desert, triumphing over temptation, before beginning to announce the good news of the Kingdom of God to all people. During the 40 days of Lent—days of repentance, of fasting and of prayer—the Christian undertakes a pilgrimage towards the Lord. He prepares to meet his Lord in the radiant night of the Resurrection, during the liturgy of Holy Pascha. Similarly, each Wednesday and each Friday, in remembrance of Christ's Passion, faithful Christians prepare for the coming Sunday, which is the day of the Resurrection—a day on which we remain in total fasting before the Liturgy, in order to be filled and nourished with the Bread of Heaven during the Holy Eucharist, that is, communion in the Holy Mysteries.

Our basic sickness is *laziness*, a laziness that persuades us that no change is possible within our life and that every effort is useless. This laziness is at the root of all sin, because it poisons our spiritual energy at its very source.

The consequence of this laziness is *discouragement*, or despair. The sense of despair represents a terrible danger for the soul, amounting to a kind of suicide. It is precisely laziness or slothfulness, together with discouragement, which create in us the desire to dominate others. This we call "lust of power." This desire to dominate—this lust for power over others—makes us look for some sort of compensation by creating a false attitude towards other people, by trying to order them about and to have some form of mastery or control over them. Such an attitude can take the form of simple indifference or even scorn. Following upon spiritual suicide, then, we come to spiritual murder. Since our slothfulness in fact makes us good for nothing, we like to believe that other people as well are simply good for nothing.

Fourthly, there are "idle words." The word can save, but it can also kill and poison. It can be the instrument of a lie and of deception. Wrenched from its divine origin and distorted, the word becomes merely empty. "Now I say to you, for every baseless or empty word spoken by men they will be called upon to render an account on the Day of Judgment" (Matthew 12:26).

Father Schmemann now moves on to more positive points concerning repentance. *Chastity*, or the spirit of integrity, means a certain sobriety that unifies the human person; it is the very opposite of that slothfulness which scatters us and makes it impossible for us to behold all things in proper perspective. Chastity recreates within us a true scale of value.

The first fruit of chastity is humility. Humility is the victory of truth over every lie. Only humility is capable of truth, of seeing and accepting things precisely as they are. Therefore it alone enables us to behold God and to behold His love in all things. This is why the Gospel tells us that God bestows His gifts upon the humble, but not upon the proud and haughty.

Man in his fallen state is impatient because he is blinded about himself. He is all too quick to judge and condemn other people. *Patience* therefore is a divine virtue. Patience is not at all some kind of fatalistic resignation, it means rather perseverance in an inner combat. God is patient.

Finally, the crown and the fruit of every virtue is *love.* Such love however can only be bestowed by God Himself. This gift is the aim and end of every spiritual effort, of every preparation, and of every form of asceticism.

All of this is summed up, then, in the third request which closes the prayer of St Ephrem: "Grant me to see my own transgressions and not to judge my brother." Pride is a great danger, but when chastity, humility, patience, and love are joined together within us as a single effective force, then the last enemy—pride—is destroyed.

We can see than that the prayer of St Ephrem is a tremendous help to us in our personal effort throughout the period of Great Lent: an effort whose purpose is to free us from certain spiritual illnesses that prevent us from turning ourselves toward God, which divide us within ourselves, and which separate us from our neighbor. At this point it would be useful to say just a few words about *metania* or prostrations. In his book, *Great Lent*, Father Schmemann also insists upon the fact that the Church never separates the soul from the body. Man in his fallen state is fallen from God, and in the whole of his life he must be restored to God.

The body is holy because God Himself "became flesh." Salvation and repentance by no means signify scorn or negligence of the body, as some people have held, but quite to the contrary. They mean the restoration of the body in its true function as the temple of the Holy Spirit. Christian asceticism is not a struggle *against* the body, but *for* it. For this reason the whole man—body and soul—are involved in repentance. Prostrations are merely signs of repentance and humiliation, of adoration and worship; therefore prostrations represent the most perfect ritual image of what Lent is all about.

14) Prayers for every moment of the day or the night (the Jesus Prayer)

Lord Jesus Christ, Son of God, have mercy upon me, a sinner

This brief prayer can situate itself in the depths of the heart, in every circumstance, whether we be working or walking in the street, whether during our free time or riding in public transportation, in moments of temptation or of particular difficulty, in other moments of decision or of seeking an answer. But this brief prayer can also serve our meditation. These words make up what is called the "prayer of the heart" or "perpetual prayer" which, in the best of circumstances, is actually prayed according to the rhythm of our breathing and of our very life. These few words enable us to fulfill St Paul's command whe he declared: "Pray without ceasing" (1 Thess 5).

C) The Psalter

The book of the Psalms, called in Hebrew the Book of Praise, was for all the of the people of the Old Covenant the most important book of prayer that they possessed. Our Lord used the Psalter in His own prayer and in His common prayers with His disciples (Mark 14:26).

For this reason the Church took up the Psalter and made it her own. Quite naturally, each liturgical service includes the reading or the singing of certain songs. Similarly, at a very early period, and with perfect continuity with the New Testament, certain Psalms have been granted a privileged place within the liturgy: they were read as prophecies of the coming mystery of Christ. This is the case with Psalm 2: "The Lord said to me: you are my son. This day I have begotten you"; Psalm 21: "My God, My God, why hast Thou abandoned me?"; Psalm 67: "Let God arise, let His enemies be scattered"; and of still many others. Finally, the Psalter has been received as a virtual school of a personal prayer by many Christian people. Inspired by the Holy Spirit, this book teaches us to speak to our God and to express to Him in simple and profound terms of thanksgiving our joy, our stress, our anxiety, and our desire to do His will and to put His Word into practice.

Unlike certain books of spirituality which present prayer in a somewhat abstract manner, cut off from the rest of life, the Psalms teach us to make every situation into an encounter with God. Whether we be tested or whether we be exulting in joy, whether we be alone or with a large number of friends, we find in the Psalms precisely that attitude that speaks to our situation. In the Psalms we learn to envision everything within the universe as a creation of God, and to praise the Lord for His creative activity. This is especially true with Psalm 103 [104] which we read at the beginning of Vespers, and which is a veritable hymn of creation. Other Psalms teach us to speak to God of our deepest sense of distress: for example, Psalm 87. Others teach us to give thanks from the depths of our heart for the distress that we know, such as Psalm 68. What other biblical text can better teach us the true meaning of repentance than the well-known Psalm 50 [51]? Other Psalms of enthronement or of kingship (such as Psalms 119 ff, and 92-99) help us to pray as members of the Church, of whom Christ is both Lord and King.

In our personal prayer we can use the Psalter in two different ways. The first consists in reading the Psalms and in praying them according to liturgical order, that is according to the so-called *"Kathismata."* The other way is to choose one Psalm or another according to our needs, that is, according to the state in which we find ourselves, in order to express aloud what the Spirit speaks within our hearts. Both manners of praying the Psalms have been practiced since the beginning of the Christian era by faithful people. The first helps us so that we do not fall into subjectivism; the second enables us to integrate into all of our daily experiences the whole prayer of Israel and of the Church. The Psalter represents the prototype of all Christian hymnography.

D) Commentary on the Lord's Prayer

1) How Jesus prayed

> *"One day," the Gospel tells us (Luke 11:1), "Jesus was praying. When He had finished praying, one of His disciples asked Him, 'Lord teach us to pray as John taught his disciples.' Jesus said to them: 'When you pray, say: Our Father . . . '"*

The Gospels often speak to us of the prayer Jesus uttered in public or in private, by day or by night, in solitude, in desert places, or on the mountainside. Jesus also prayed at particular moments when important events were about to happen: at His Baptism in the Jordan (Luke 3:21); before calling the twelve disciples (Luke 6:12); before Simon Peter's confession of the divinity of Jesus (Luke 9:18); at the time of the transfiguration of Jesus on Mt Tabor (Luke 9:28); at the resurrection of His friend Lazarus (John 11:41); during and after the Last Supper in the Upper Room (Luke 22:19 and John 17); during His agony in the garden of Gethsemane; upon the cross; at the breaking of bread after the resurrection; and at the time of His ascension into heaven (Luke 24). One could give many other examples of moments when Jesus prayed.

We would highly recommend the following exercise: Read with great attention the four Gospels and notice all of the texts that speak of Jesus at prayer, of His teaching about prayer, of the importance of prayer, of the relationship between prayer and whole of the Christian life turned toward God, and of the relationship between prayer, fasting, and mercy. Such an exercise teaches us a great many things. We notice particularly that the evangelist Luke paid the closest attention to the moments when Jesus was in prayer at different moments in His public ministry.

We discover that the prayer of Jesus Himself is realized in the power of the Holy Spirit. We can even say that it is by the Holy Spirit that Jesus prays, and that it is the Spirit Himself that prays in Jesus. We ourselves from time to time have a very modest experience of that interior voice that resounds within us, that beats in unison with the beating of our heart, and that fills us with joy and with love, both of God and His creation.

According to the Gospels, Jesus prayed. Now if for holy people prayer became a continual state—a flame of love and of praise which burned within their very heart—can we not imagine to what extent in Jesus' own life prayer penetrated the whole of His existence? Jesus was wholly filled with prayer, ceaselessly and fully turned toward His Father, speaking with Him in a language of praise and intercession, in an intimacy that goes infinitely beyond anything we can imagine or experience as human beings.

It is important to add as well that the prayer of Jesus is by no means limited to the time of His earthly life. Jesus promises to His disciples that He will intercede for them before the Father: "It is better for you that I go away . . . I will pray the Father and He will give you another Comforter" (John 16:7 and 14:16). We know that this heavenly intercession that Jesus makes on behalf of men is a permanent one. As the Epistle to the Hebrews tells us (7:25), "He lives forever to intercede on their behalf." The prayer of the Church, the Body of Christ—that is, the prayer of all believers—is deeply united with the prayer of the resurrected Christ. In her praise and her intercession, the Church is drawn into the very prayer of her Master, for the prayer of Christ embraces and undergirds all of our petitions.

Therefore, in order for us to discover the deep meaning of Jesus' teaching about prayer, we must enter into the framework of His own prayer—into that most intimate, permanent and universal prayer which He offers without ceasing to God the Father. It is in this framework that we can best understand the meaning of the petitions that make up that we call the Lord's Prayer. The Lord's Prayer can be divided into four parts:

1. The invocation: Our Father who art in heaven.
2. The three first requests concerning the coming of the Kingdom among men.
3. The three last requests concerning man, his needs, his sin, and his temptations.
4. The final praise of God.

2) *The invocation "Our Father"*

What Jesus communicated to His disciples, and through them to all men, is not simply a prayer among others, but the most extraordinary secret of His whole life, a secret that troubled so many of His contemporaries because it seemed to violate their most traditional practices of prayer. Jesus revealed to His friends the very name of God: Father. This name, only the Son could pronounce; only Jesus *knows* that God is His Father. This is the word or title which is constantly in Jesus' heart and on His lips: Father. In Aramaic, the language which Jesus Himself and His disciples spoke, the name Father is rendered by "Abba." This word signifies "Father," but it does so in a very intimate way. Its closest equivalent in American English would be "Daddy." Now any Jew who was a contemporary of Jesus would never have dreamed of calling God Daddy or Abba. This would have been simply blasphemous; it would have been scandalous; it would even have indicated some form of mental instability on the part of the one who uttered that name. Jesus, however, had no fear of scandal. The word Abba came forth spontaneously from His heart to His lips, and that from His earliest childhood, from the very moment at which His human consciousness began to mature (Luke 2:49).

Jesus commanded His disciples to pray. He transmitted and gave to them the name Abba or Father. We can imagine a deeply united family which receives an orphan into its midst. The new child is embraced with tenderness and affection by its adopted family, and little by little it becomes accustomed to its new home and feels itself to be thoroughly welcomed. A day comes when, overflowing with a feeling of affection, the son of the family tells his newfound friend, draping his arm around his shoulder: "I want you to call my parents Mommy and Daddy. Everything I own is yours as well; I give it all to you." In the Gospels we can also discover this extraordinary love of Jesus for all men whom He considered His brethren, and whom He seeks to lead home to His own Father: "Father I wish that there where I am they should be also with Me . . . in order that the love with which You have loved Me might be in them and I might be in them" (John 17:24-26).

That man is an orphan who finds himself lost in a distant land, and the road leading back home towards the Father is long and difficult. Let us re-read the parable of the Prodigal Son in Luke 15, verses 11-32. There Jesus shows us just how fully sin creates a distance between man and God, how sin draws man into distant lands where he comes to know hardship and suffering, discouragement and sadness. His return to the house of the Father leads him across a difficult road. How could the man possibly make such a journey if the Father Himself, beholding him from far off, did not run to meet him and throw His arms about him? The great Dutch painter Rembrandt illustrated this marvelous scene in an unforgettable way.

The Lord's Prayer is always in danger of being trivialized in the daily prayer of modern Christians. In the ancient Church it was taught and explained to adults who were preparing themselves for baptism, those who were called catechumens. This teaching on the Lord's Prayer came only at the end of a long period of education, after the actual baptism itself.

This means that it is only at the end of a long roadway of questing, necessitating a deep and thoroughgoing conversion of the heart, that God reveals Himself truly as Father. As long as our heart is closed, the name Father can scarcely be pronounced. When God is distant, how can we possibly pray with any truth or any semblance of reality?

Nevertheless, Jesus knows man's weakness. "He searches into the depth of our hearts and of our inner being," the Scriptures tell us. All through the Gospels we find indications of how we are to make this journey into prayer. The Spirit Himself teaches us, and communicates to us little by little, until finally prayer fills us to overflowing. The most living prayer, the deepest prayer, the most personal prayer, is that which rises ceaselessly within the heart of Jesus Himself. It is this prayer which is called of the Spirit. The Spirit is prayer, and this Spirit is in Jesus as a source of Living Water. And this source brings forth ever again within Jesus the name of the Father, Abba. This same source is within ourselves as well, but it has been obstructed, polluted by our sins, our ignorances, our refusals (John 7:37-39). "Give us always this water," we beg with the Samaritan woman at the well of Jacob (John 4:15). Give us always

Thy Spirit. Jesus promises us the gift of the Spirit whom He will send from the Father. St Paul declares that God has sent into our hearts the Spirit of His Son, who cries: Abba, Father (Galatians 4:6). From the time of Pentecost, the Holy Spirit dwells within the world like living water that quenches our thirst for God, like a fire which kindles and enlightens our very being: "I have come to cast fire upon the earth," says Jesus, "and how I wish that it were already lighted!" (Luke 12:49).

The Spirit of Jesus opens to us the heart of our Master. He reveals to us the depths of His burning love for us. The life of the Church is nothing other than a ceaseless invitation, ceaseless invocation to the Spirit, that He might descend and dwell within us. It is precisely then, when the Spirit is present in the eucharistic community of the Church following the consecration of the bread and wine, that "we dare with faith and without condemnation to call upon the heavenly God as Father and to say: Our Father . . .''

In the Church the prayer of Jesus (My Father) broadens to embrace the whole of the human family (Our Father), who find there shelter within the heart of the Master Himself. In the Spirit of Jesus who dwells within the Church, in a continuing Pentecost, men and women rediscover fraternal love. Human love, even if it is deformed, is a reflection—often an unconscious one—of the love of God. Only God is Love (1 John 4:8, 16). Further on we shall discover just how demanding our love can be of all of human relations.

Our Father

When this cry, "Our Father," rises up within the heart of a person, that person rediscovers his true personal identity. Everyone without exception was created to become a child of God, a unique child, a beloved child, made in the image and likeness of the Only Son, the Beloved Jesus Christ Himself. This is why the love of God knows no bounds. The Gospel of Jesus Christ, therefore, resembles a net that God has thrown over the entire world in order to draw all men into eternal life. We should also remember that the Lord's Prayer was first of all prayed by Jesus together with His disciples. It takes more than a simple meeting of a few persons to be able to call upon the name of God and address Him as "Our Father." The Lord Himself is always present in this prayer, which is both communal and ecclesial by its very nature. For this prayer is always an extension of the prayer of the unique Son of God, which reaches out to all persons at all times within human history.

Our Father Who Art In Heaven (Matthew 6:9)

In the Gospel of St Luke, the formula is shorter and more to the point: "Father" (Luke 11:2).

We should not be surprised by the differences that appear in the writings of the various evangelists. In its public prayer the Church has shown a definite preference for the more elaborate form of the Lord's Prayer given to us by the tradition of St Matthew. The tradition of St. Luke, however, is also of very great antiquity. Most likely, Jesus often transmitted to His disciples the words of the Lord's Prayer, either in a direct way as we see Him doing in the Gospels, or else by offering it with more elaboration and development in the context of an explanation of traditional Jewish prayers. Therefore, the various differences in formulation are quite natural and even necessary, if the teaching is to be living and continually growing. *living, faithful tradition*

Our Father Who Art In Heaven

This is the usual way for Jesus to speak of the Father. We should not see in this formula any kind of a limitation placed upon the reign of Him who is the creator both of heaven and of earth. "The earth is the Lord's and the fullness thereof, the world and those who dwell therein" (Psalm 23[24]:1).

This manner of recalling the celestial dwelling place of God is quite traditional in Jewish prayer. It is useful for us even today to situate mankind and the world as a whole in their true perspective: the perspective of a vertical relationship relative to Him who "dwells in inaccessible light" (1 Timothy 6:16), beyond every limit of our

earthly horizons. Jewish piety was, and remains today, highly
sensitive to what we call the "transcendence" of God, that is, to His
being which is beyond all of our conceptions, words, and rational
perception.

But what is radically new in comparison to traditional Jewish
prayer in this formulation that Jesus gives to prayer addressed to
His Father, is the fact that an infinite distance between heaven and
earth has been crossed and eliminated by the "descent" of the Son
of God upon the earth through His incarnation, and by the
"ascension" of the Son of Man toward the Father. From the time
of His ascension in the person of the glorified Jesus ("God is with
us," Emmanuel) Jesus says: "If anyone loves me he will keep my word
and my Father will love him and we shall come to him, and we shall
take up our dwelling in him" (John 14:23).

In addition, the designation "heaven" recalls to us the infinite and
marvelous destiny of every man, which is to be shaped according to
the image of the divine Trinity. In the words of St Paul, "our citizen-
ship is in the heavens" (Philippians 3:20). This orientation toward
heaven recalls to us our true vocation and our true destiny. "Let us
lift up our hearts," declares the priest in the eucharistic liturgy, just
before the consecration of the Holy Gifts. This elevation of our heart
signifies a return to our true and ultimate homeland, to the heaven
which is situated within ourselves; and it means a return after a long
and tragic exile. This return to our ultimate dwelling place in the
Kingdom of God by no means signifies any kind of scorn or rejection
of earthly existence. It means rather that we come to discover "the
one thing necessary," the very treasure of our life, towards which
our heart aspires, a goal which enlightens our very existence and all
of our work upon this earth.

3) The coming of the Kingdom of God

**Hallowed be Thy name, Thy Kingdom come, Thy will be
done on earth as it is heaven**

Unlike the following requests that express human misery and

human need, these initial affirmations could very well be expressed by Jesus Himself in the context of His own personal prayer. In these words, the Jewish prayer with which Jesus was nourished from His childhood and which rises spontaneously to His lips is summarized and fully expressed. This is a summary of a Jewish prayer lived by Jesus, but one that is infinitely transcended by His own personal prayer. These three requests summarize the entire revelation of the Old Covenant: the sanctification of the Name of the Lord on Mt Sinai, the first manifestation of the Kingdom of God on earth, a quest to discover the will of God through meditation upon the divine law.

Hallowed be thy name

The revelation and the hallowing of the Name of God constitutes the most basic message from God to His elect people: "You will obey my commandments," teaches the law of Moses, "you will practice my laws, I am the Lord. He will not profane my holy Name, in order that I might be sanctified within the midst of the children of Israel, I, the Lord, who sanctifies you" (cf. Leviticus 22:31-2).

The Name of God is profaned by the disobedience and unfaithfulness of His people, His bride, whom God chose and loved. God hallows His Name by transforming the human heart: "I will sanctify my great Name which has been profaned among the nations . . . I will draw you out among the nations . . . I will give you a new heart . . . and you will be my people, and I shall be your God" (Ezekiel 36:20-28).

The Name of God is one with the person that it designates and whom it manifests. When God reveals Himself, He reveals His Name. To praise and adore God means to glorify His Holy Name in the only true temple in which genuine praise of God can be offered, that is, within the human heart. Nevertheless, the Name of God is unutterable. The heart of man could not contain this Name if God Himself had not placed his Name within that heart, if the human heart of God made man had not once and for all become the receptacle of the divine presence. In the words of St Paul, "In Him, all the fullness of divinity dwelt bodily" (Colossians 2:9).

The Name of God which flows forth from the Gospel revelation is threefold and unique:

1. "Father, I have revealed to them thy Name" (John 17:6, 26). What is new above all in the revelation of Jesus to His disciples, and through them to the world, is precisely this name of Father, "Abba," who relates Himself to us in deep intimacy, yet whose Name remains ineffable and ultimately inaccessible.

2. But to speak in this way of the Father, to turn to Him with such deep confidence, means that we must discover ourselves to be both children and sons of God. The Name of the Father is revealed in the name of Jesus, which means "God saves." This is the name which the angel announced to the Virgin in Nazareth; it is the name which Mary contemplated within her own heart as she listened to the new life which was conceived and grew within her womb. It is the same name that she spoke again and again, even to the moment of her Son's agony in Golgotha. It is the name of her Son and her God, the name "before which every knee in heaven and on the earth and under the earth will bow" (Phil 2:10). The name of Jesus is the name of the glorified Lord, by which the apostles accomplished miracles, which the martyrs confessed publicly, murmuring it in secret or aloud at the moment of their death. The first Christians were therefore called "those who invoke the name of the Lord" (Acts 9:14, 21; 1 Cor 1:2; etc).

3. The divine Name is filled with the Spirit of God, the Comforter, in whom every word and every name becomes both true and living.

The Name of God is a light that touches me at the deepest level of my existence. It awakens me and gives me life. Thy Name, O Lord, is Justice, Love, Wisdom, Tenderness, Peace, Holiness, Light, Gentleness. When I hallow thine Name, my heart is enlightened and burns with the rays of thine eternal Sun. I am alive, and I pass without difficulty through the black waters of death:

"For thy name's sake, O Lord, grant me to live in thy righteousness. Lift up my soul from oppression . . . for I am Thy servant" (Psalm 142[143]: 11-12).

The Christian hears the Seer of the Book of Revelation as he transmits the words that the Spirit addresses to the churches: "I will inscribe upon him the name of my God . . . the new name that I bear . . . and I shall never blot out his name from the book of life" (Revelation 3:12, 5).

Hallowed Be Thy Name

May this prayer rise up without ceasing from the depths of our heart. Through the praise of men and women, creation itself glorifies and calls upon its Creator: "Let every breath praise the Lord!" May we all learn once again the language of praise! In Jesus, the human heart has already brought about a reconciliation between earth and heaven: "Father, I have manifested Thy name to men; I have glorified Thee upon the earth, I have finished the work that Thou gavest me to do" (John 17:4, 6). In Jesus, all is fulfilled. In Him the holiness of the Name of God has been restored.

Thy Kingdom Come

The Chosen People of God awaited the coming of the Kingdom at the end of time. The more difficult their trials became, the more impatient and ardent became their way of looking forward toward the manifestation of the Kingdom of God.

The Gospels tell us "the Kingdom of God has drawn near" (Mark 1:15). John the Baptist cried out: "Repent!" And after him, Jesus also declared, "Repent, for the Kingdom of God is at hand." To hallow the Name of God is to bring the Kingdom ever more quickly, to manifest its presence, to inaugurate it within our hearts, to submit our lives to it, and to conform our will to it in all things.

Nevertheless, Jesus declares to Pilate: "The Kingdom of God is not of this world." Pilate points to Jesus and declares with irony, "Behold your king!" The execution of Jesus upon the infamous cross can only hasten the manifestation of the Kingdom of God: "Glorify Thy son," Jesus prays before His Passion, "so that the Son might glorify Thee." On the cross all things are fulfilled, the prince of this world is cast out: "I saw Satan fall from heaven like lightning" (Luke 10:18).

The Kingdom of God does not come with violence: "Behold my servant whom I have chosen . . . I will pour out upon him my Spirit. He will not break a bent reed, and a smoking wick he will not extinguish" (Matthew 12:18-20, quoting Isaiah 41:1-3). The Kingdom of God is manifested within the inner life, by the fruits of the Spirit: gentleness, patience, wisdom, love. The Spirit asks Himself: "Upon whom shall I dwell, if not upon him who is gentle, him who is humble and who fears my words?" (Isaiah 66:2). Thus it is quite clear that the Kingdom of God belongs to those who bear the Spirit within themselves: "Blessed are the meek, for they shall inherit the earth."

An ancient variant reading in the Gospel of St Luke replaces the words "Thy Kingdom come" by the following request: "May Thy Holy Spirit come upon us and purify us." All the gifts of the Kingdom, all the most intimate and abundant life of the divine Trinity, is constituted and focused by the coming of the Spirit, the Paraclete or Comforter. It is this Spirit whom we call upon in the liturgies as well as in our most intimate prayer: "Send down Thy Holy Spirit upon us and upon the gifts here set forth."

Thy Will Be Done On Earth As It Is In Heaven

By tasting the forbidden fruit in the Garden of Eden, man distanced himself from God, rejected the divine love, and opposed to the will of God his own human desires and illusions. An unbridgeable gulf was thereby created between God and man. The world has cut itself off from the very sources of its life: the garden has become a barren desert (cf Isaiah: 42:6). The will of God the Father is a loving will, one of life and of freedom. The entire life of Jesus is one marked by a ceaseless "Yes!" spoken to the Father: in Him all was "Yes and Amen" (2 Corinthians 1:19). Jesus' own will is always perfect agreement with the will of the Father. "I did not come to accomplish my own will but the will of my Father who is in heaven" (John 5:30). Jesus refuses to obey His own will, paying for his obedience the price of his blood-filled drops of sweat in the Garden of Gethsemane: "Not my will, but Thine be done." In Jesus' own struggle and agony, the human will is put to death. At the same time, that will is healed and regenerated from within by the breath of the Spirit of love. Our will, finally, can coincide with and identify with the will of the Father, without our being either destroyed or crushed. To the degree that the Spirit works in our hearts, we acquire the very "mind" of Jesus (Philippians 2:5). We acquire His own will, His wisdom, His love, His Spirit. Obedience to God no longer forced; it is a response to an interior law of the heart. It becomes an expression of our deepest, most free, and most loving being.

When the heart of man opens to his Creator, the entire earth also finds its deliverance and reconciliation. Man therefore may be described as both a lever and a fulcrum by which the Holy Spirit accomplishes his saving work within the world.

On Earth As In Heaven

Here again we discover this ceaseless movement of descent and of ascension. The entire destiny of man consists in unifying these two extremities of the divine creation: to reconcile earth and heaven by rendering the earth transparent and radiant.

4) The Needs Of Sinful Men

Give Us This Day Our Daily Bread, and Forgive Us Our Trespasses, As We Forgive Those Who Trespass Against Us. And Lead Us Not Into Temptation, But Deliver Us From Evil

In the preceding requests, Jesus introduces His brethren—all mankind—into a life of praise offered to the Father. This praise focuses upon the Name of God and upon His Kingdom. Thereby Jesus teaches us to unite our will with the will of God. From the moment of His incarnation, Jesus identifies Himself with human persons, and through Him their most vital requests rise to the Father: "All that you ask the Father in my name will be granted to you." Jesus takes upon Himself our needs and our weaknesses, He knows how very fragile we are. Our sorrows and our sins are received within the very heart of the Lamb, who took upon Himself the sin of the world, and who "has been tested in every way as we are only without sin" (Hebrews 4:15). These last three requests express in the most explicit way possible the radical newness of the gospel.

Give Us This Day Our Daily Bread

The usual translation of this request concerning bread fails to render in a truly satisfactory way the original meaning of Jesus' words. Our daily bread: what does this refer to? Is it in fact the bread of each day, produced by the work and the struggle of men? Does it refer to earthly nourishment that man needs to feed himself, to clothe himself, and simply to maintain his physical existence? At last, we are told, we are placing our feet upon the ground; the Church is beginning to consider the true needs of men and their daily nourishment. At last the Churches are becoming concerned about human justice . . .

As important as that concern may be, this particular petition of the Lord's Prayer would be tragically impoverished if we were to see in it only a concern for earthly needs. Of course it is true that Jesus multiplied bread in order to nourish the hungry crowd in the desert. Of course it is true that Jesus transformed water into wine at the wedding at Cana in order to give joy to the participants of the wedding feast. Nevertheless, we must reread the Gospels with genuine attentiveness, in order to discover in them the real meaning of "bread." The bread of the earth is not man's only need. In the desert, Jesus Himself rejects the Satanic temptation to transform stones into bread: "Man does not live by bread alone, but by every word that comes forth from the mouth of God" (Matthew 4:4). Whereas the first man fed himself from the forbidden fruit, the Son of Man replies to his sinful act by fasting in the desert. Hunger and thirst experienced by Jesus point beyond human food to essential divine nourishment: "I have another food that you do not know. My food is to do the will of Him who sent me" (John 4:32-34). In Jesus, bread and the will of the Father are one and the same. The most material and most earthly of all of Jesus' miracles, in which He multiplied bread to feed the crowd, also marks the moment of His most rich and profound teaching on the meaning of the true Bread of Life. We should reread with great attentiveness Chapter 6 of the Gospel of St John, verses 26-66. Aren't we often like these people who sought Jesus out along the coast of the Sea of Galilee, "not because you have seen signs, but because you ate your fill of bread? Work not for perishable food, but for the food which abides unto eternal life" (John 6: 26-27). The rest of this discussion that Jesus offers to the crowd shows just how this "food which abides unto eternal life" is nothing other than the very life of God that Jesus communicates to us. This He can do, since He Himself is the living Bread which comes down from heaven: "I am the Bread of Life . . . whoever eats this Bread will live forever" (John 6:51).

The true Bread transforms him who consumes it into the very likeness of his Creator. In the eucharist the bread of men becomes a food of immortality; the heavenly Bread gives life to our immortal bodies and souls.

The expression "daily bread" must be clearly understood. Literally the expression means "that bread which is to come," the bread of tomorrow. The expression, therefore, means no longer "daily bread" in its usual mundane sense. It means rather "our bread of tomorrow," that is, the bread of the coming of the Kingdom of God, the bread of life, the word of God, the will of the Father, the coming of the Holy Spirit. The fact that this expression refers also to the coming of the Spirit is suggested by Jesus Himself when He offers to His disciples His first explanation of the Lord's Prayer: "If you who are evil know how to give good things to your children, how much more will the heavenly Father give the Holy Spirit to those who ask Him?" (Luke 11:13).

The Holy Spirit sums up within Himself every need of men. In Him there is no longer any separation between what is spiritual and what is earthly. Every domain of human existence is blessed, every need is known, and no particular food is impure any longer. All belongs to man, just as man belongs to God: "Seek first the Kingdom of God and His righteousness, and all the rest will be added to you" (Matthew 6:33).

"Give us today our daily bread, the bread of life, the bread of the heavenly banquet." This request, however, in no way neglects human need. It includes in itself the bread of every day as well as the sanctification of every day. Therefore it meets every need of our existence, no matter how concrete or simple that need may be. Our most humble, hidden, or neglected needs are also met by God's gift: in the words of St Irenaeus, "the glory of God is man in the fullness of life." Such a man is filled with the Spirit of God.

And Forgive Us Our Debts, As We Forgive Our Debtors

The so-called "ecumenical" translation of the Lord's Prayer reads, "forgive us our trespasses as we forgive those who trespass against us." It is important, however, to rediscover the original meaning of this word as it appears in the Gospel. The image of debt and debtor is a frequent one in Jesus' parables. The teaching concerning it is twofold:

1. All good works and efforts of man are themselves insignificant and inadequate for paying back the debt which is ours before God. The parable of the debtor in Matthew 18:23-35, makes this abundantly clear. The only way to avoid condemnation at the Last Judgment is to find some means to make amends for this debt. Jesus reveals to us that the heavenly Father is a God of mercy, who loves the world, who seeks not the death of the sinner, but that the sinner should repent and live.

2. The conditions of our acquittal by God are that we forgive others the debts that they owe to us. Jesus teaches His disciples the difficult lesson of forgiving sins and of loving their enemies. Here we find ourselves at the very heart of the Gospel. The forgiveness of sins is the fundamental criterion and the fullest revelation of true love; it is the sure sign of the presence of the Spirit within us: "Be merciful, as your heavenly Father is merciful" (Luke 6:36).

Forgiving those who have offended us is a necessary precondition and ground of all our prayer, of the interior sacrifice of our heart, and of the offering to God of our very life. At the moment of His own supreme sacrifice upon the cross, Jesus prayed for those who crucified Him: "My Father, forgive them; they know not what they do" (Luke 23:34). We find this same word of forgiveness on the lips of St Stephen when he was being stoned to death: "Lord do not hold this sin against them" (Acts 7:60). Man needs God's forgiveness in order to live, since man's sinfulness draws him away from God. God longs for man's repentance; He longs for man's love (the Prodigal Son). "Give me your heart," says God, "and I will satisfy your deepest thirst."

Certain manuscripts include in the Lord's Prayer the request, "forgive us our debts as we have already forgiven those who are indebted to us." This form in the past tense underscores the very real and precise fulfillment of an act which is necessary in order to receive God's forgiveness, to enter into a deep and personal relationship with Him, and to receive the power of His Holy Spirit. This reality of God's forgiveness makes itself felt especially before eucharistic communion and liturgical praise. The forgiveness of sins is the necessary foundation for a life that seeks to enter into the Kingdom of the Holy Trinity, a Kingdom inaugurated by the Holy Eucharist.

And Lead Us Not Into Temptation, But Deliver Us From Evil

Literally this reads: "Lead us not into temptation but deliver us from the Evil One." We should note that the Gospel of St Luke omits the second part of this request.

This is basically a request for protection. We find ourselves troubled at times by the words of this prayer, because we often feel it implies that God Himself leads us into temptation. The apostle James, however, warns us against any such interpretation: "No one under trial or temptation should say, 'I am being tempted by God'; for God is untouched by evil, and does not Himself tempt anyone" (James 1:13).

No man is totally free from temptation. Jesus Himself warns us against the arrows and the nets of the Evil One, that is Satan: "Simon,

Simon, beware! It has been granted to Satan to sift each of you like wheat; but I have prayed for you that your faith may not fail" (Luke 22:31-32). The allusion here is not simply to relatively minor temptations of daily life, but above all to the fundamental temptation of the Christian who lives in a world enslaved to the Beast, a temptation that places the Christian's faithfulness to God into serious question. Nevertheless, this kind of testing is necessary; and the Holy Spirit Himself leads us through it, just as He led Jesus into the desert to be tempted there by the devil (see Matthew 4:1). Jesus' prayer for Peter prophetically announces the coming night of His own Passion, the moment in which Jesus Himself will be tested by a feeling of utter abandonment, solitude and evil. Jesus is preparing His disciples for this ultimate confrontation; beyond abandonment and renunciation, they will discover the forgiveness and infinite love of God.

Similarly, believers are called to take up the struggle of our Savior Himself against the Satanic powers which enslave the world. This is a murderous and thankless combat. Nevertheless, the power of life in the risen Lord enables us to confront the Enemy, despite his inplacable hatred and his determination to destroy the original beauty of God's creation. If such struggle is necessary, if temptation by the Evil One is inevitable, "God is faithful and He will not allow you to be tested above your powers; but when the temptation comes He will provide for you a way out, thereby enabling you to endure it" (1 Cor 10:13). This warfare, undertaken in the name of Christ, demands ceaseless vigilance and total confidence in the power of the Spirit who dwells within our mortal bodies: "Be awake and watch! your adversary the devil, like a roaring lion, is prowling around seeking someone to devour. Resist him, firm in the faith, knowing that the same suffering has been given to your brethren in the world" (1 Peter 5:8-9). We learn to wage this supreme struggle through the events of every day, in our faithfulness to little things. "Whoever is faithful in little, is faithful also in much" (Luke 16:10).

Faithfulness in testing is the "good combat" that we wage in imitation of Christ. Jesus' victory over the forces of evil is manifested in the scandal of the cross. And to us the Spirit of God says: "Remain faithful unto death, and I will give you the crown of life" (Revelation 2:10).

5) *Final Praise Of The Holy Trinity*

For Thine Is The Kingdom And The Power And The Glory Forever And Ever. Amen

This passage is one of liturgical praise, inherited from Jewish prayer, that has been transmitted to us from the earliest generations of the Church. It leads us in our study of the Lord's Prayer back to our starting point. Praise of the divine Trinity is both the starting point and the culmination of all Christian prayer (the Orthodox liturgy uses in place of its final benediction a trinitarian formula: "For Thine is the Kingdom and the Power and the Glory of the Father and of the Son and of the Holy Spirit . . ."). Such praise undergirds our whole existence and fills all of our requests. By it we express our deepest, most disinterested love, together with our perfect adoration of God. Such expressions of praise were very frequent in the early Church, as becomes clear to us when we read the mysterious book of Revelation, which contains vestiges of ancient liturgical formulas in use in the churches of Asia Minor. There we find striking passages on the praise offered by every creature to "Him who is on the Throne and to the Lamb."

"Then I heard every created thing in heaven and on earth and under the earth and in the sea, all that is in them, crying: 'Praise and honor, glory and might, to Him who sits on the Throne and to the Lamb, for ever and ever!' And the four living creatures said, Amen!" (Revelation 5:13; see also 7:12 and 11:15).

The conclusion of the Lord's Prayer fits well into this overall liturgical tradition. If we remember the central place that the Lord's Prayer has in our eucharistic celebration, between the consecration of the gifts and the communion itself, we can see that this expression of praise exults above all the coming of the Kingdom of Christ which He shares with the Father and the Holy Spirit. The coming of the Spirit in the Eucharist of the Church makes of this coming divine

Kingdom a present reality. At the end of time, the Lord will only manifest His Kingdom in visible form.

Power and glory are the ineffable radiance of the royal presence of Christ within the world. In this present age, God willingly limits His power in the presence of our human freedom. God does not force man to love Him. The only power by which our heart can be opened to grace and to the light of God is the power of love itself.

The glory of God remains hidden within our bodies of clay. To offer glory to God is to acknowledge His infinite authority, His sovereignty, in the only place where God could not reign without our consent: that is, within our own heart. When the heart is willing, God fills it and embraces our whole life with His glory; He enables it to partake of divine life and to inherit the fullness of His Kingdom.

The Church of Christ is the locus, the privileged place of the Divine Presence. It is in the Church that communion in the life of the Holy Trinity is offered to mankind. The Kingdom of God draws near and becomes a reality only through the struggle and the victory of the saints. From this present moment, each of us is called to participate in that struggle, in the warfare accomplished by God's holy ones. The "Amen!" which the community pronounces at the conclusion of the Lord's Prayer confirms our unconditional "yes!" at the coming of Christ, in the power of the Holy Spirit, to men and women of our own day and age.

Musical Examples

Illustrations
*Reproductions in color

Index

Bibliography

CHURCH HISTORY

J. M. Hussey. *The Orthodox Church in the Byzantine Empire.* New York: Oxford University Press, 1985.

John Meyendorff. *The Byzantine Legacy in the Orthodox Church.* Crestwood: St Vladimir's Seminary Press, 1982.

John Meyendorff. *The Orthodox Church: Its Past and Its Role in the World Today.* Crestwood: St Vladimir's Seminary Press, 1981.

Dimitri Obolensky. *The Byzantine Commonwealth.* Crestwood: St Vladimir's Seminary Press, 1982.

Alexander Schmemann. *The Historical Road of Eastern Orthodoxy.* Lydia Kesich (trans). Crestwood: St Vladimir's Seminary Press, 1977.

Constance Tarasar (ed). *Orthodox America 1794-1976.* New York: Orthodox Church in America, 1985.

Timothy Ware. *The Orthodox Church.* New York: Viking Penguin, 1963.

HYMNOGRAPHY AND MUSIC

Dimitri Conomos. *Byzantine Hymnography and Byzantine Chant.* Brookline: Holy Cross Press, 1984.

David Drillock, Helen Erickson, and John Erickson. *The Divine Liturgy* (Music). Crestwood: St Vladimir's Seminary Press, 1982.

David Drillock, Helen Erickson, and John Erickson. *Holy Week, Volume 1* (Music). Crestwood: St Vladimir's Seminary Press, 1980.

David Drillock, Helen Erickson, and John Erickson. *Holy Week, Volume 2* (Music). Crestwood: St Vladimir's Seminary Press, 1983.

David Drillock, Helen Erickson and John Erickson. *Pascha: The Resurrection of Christ* (Music). Crestwood: St Vladimir's Seminary Press, 1980.

Savas J Savas. *The Treasury of Orthodox Hymnography: Triodion.* Minneapolis: Light and Life, 1984.

Nicholas Uspensky. *Evening Worship in the Orthodox Church.* Paul Lazor (trans). Crestwood: St Vladimir's Seminary Press, 1985.

Johann von Gardner. *Russian Church Singing, Volume 1: Orthodox Worship and Hymnography.* V Morosan (trans). Crestwood: St Vladimir's Seminary Press, 1980.

ICONOGRAPHY

John Baggley and Richard Temple. *Doors of Perception: Icons and their Significance.* Crestwood: St Vladimir's Seminary Press, 1988.

St John of Damascus. *On the Divine Images.* David Anderson (trans). Crestwood: St Vladimir's Seminary Press, 1980.

Constantine D Kalokyris. *The Essence of Orthodox Iconography.* Peter Chamberas (trans). Brookline: Holy Cross Press, 1985.

Leonid Ouspensky. *Theology of the Icon, Volume 1.* Crestwood: St Vladimir's Seminary Press, 1978.

Leonid Ouspensky and Vladimir Lossky. *The Meaning of Icons,* revised edition. Crestwood: St Vladimir's Seminary Press, 1980.

St Theodore the Studite. *On the Holy Icons.* Katherine Roth (trans). Crestwood: St Vladimir's Seminary Press, 1981.

LITURGY AND SACRAMENTS

The Divine Liturgy according to St John Chrysostom, second edition. South Canaan: St Tikhon's Seminary Press, 1977.

The Divine Liturgy of St John Chrysostom (Greek and English). Brookline: Holy Cross Press, 1985.

Isabel Florence Hapgood. *Service Book of the Holy Orthodox-Catholic Apostolic Church,* revised edition. Englewood: Antiochian Orthodox Christian Archdiocese, 1983.

Festal Menaion. Mother Mary and Archimandrite Kallistos Ware (trans and ed). London: Faber and Faber, 1969.

Stanley S Harakas. *Living the Liturgy.* Minneapolis: Light and Life, 1974.

St John the Baptist Monastery. *The Orthodox Liturgy.* London: Oxford University Press, 1982.

Lenten Triodion. Mother Mary and Archimandrite Kallistos Ware (trans and ed). London: Faber and Faber, 1978.

A Manual of Eastern Orthodox Prayers. Crestwood: St Vladimir's Seminary Press, 1983.

Archbishop Paul of Finland. *The Feast of Faith: An Invitation to the Love Feast of the Kingdom of God.* Crestwood: St Vladimir's Seminary Press, 1988.

Alexander Schmemann. *The Eucharist: Sacrament of the Kingdom.* Paul Kachur (trans). Crestwood: St Vladimir's Seminary Press, 1988.

Alexander Schmemann. *For the Life of the World. Sacraments and Orthodoxy.* Crestwood: St Vladimir's Seminary Press, 1970.

For Lent, Holy Week, and the Feasts see the service books published by the Department of Religious Education (DRE) of the Orthodox Church in America, Syosset, NY.

SCRIPTURE

Georges A Barrois. *The Face of Christ in the Old Testament.* Crestwood: St Vladimir's Seminary Press, 1974.

Georges A Barrois. *Scripture Readings in Orthodox Worship.* Crestwood: St Vladimir's Seminary Press, 1977.

John Breck. *The Power of the Word: Holy Scripture in Orthodox Interpretation, Confession and Celebration.* Crestwood: St Vladimir's Seminary Press, 1986.

George Cronk. *The Message of the Bible: An Orthodox Christian Perspective.* Crestwood: St Vladimir's Seminary Press, 1982.

Thomas Hopko. *Bible and Church History, Volume III of The Orthodox Faith.* New York: Department of Religious Education, Orthodox Church in America, 1976.

Veselin Kesich. *The First Day of the New Creation: The Resurrection and the Christian Faith.* Crestwood: St Vladimir's Seminary Press, 1981.

Paul Tarazi. *I Thessalonians: A Commentary.* Crestwood: St Vladimir's Seminary Press, 1982.

Demetrius Trakatellis. *Authority and Passion: Christological Aspects of the Gospel According to Mark.* Brookline: Holy Cross Press, 1987.

THEOLOGY

Mother Alexandra. *The Holy Angels.* Minneapolis: Light and Life, 1987.

Sergius Bulgakov. *The Orthodox Church.* Crestwood: St Vladimir's Seminary Press, 1988.

Anthony M Coniaris. *Eastern Orthodoxy: A Way of Life.* Minneapolis: Light and Life, 1966.

Anthony M Coniaris. *Orthodoxy: A Creed for Today.* Minneapolis: Light and Life, 1972.

Christoforas Stavropoulos. *Partakers of the Divine Nature.* Stanley Harakas (trans). Minneapolis: Light and Life, 1976.

Stanley S Harakas. *Toward Transfigured Life.* Minneapolis: Light and Life, 1983.

Thomas Hopko. *Doctrine, Volume I of The Orthodox Faith.* New York: Department of Religious Education, Orthodox Church in America, 1976.

Vladimir Lossky. *In the Image and Likeness of God.* Crestwood: St Vladimir's Seminary Press, 1978.

Vladimir Lossky. *Orthodox Theology: An Introduction.* Crestwood: St Vladimir's Seminary Press, 1978.

John Meyendorff. *Byzantine Theology: Historical Trends and Doctrinal Themes.* New York: Fordham University Press, 1974.

Archbishop Paul of Finland. *The Faith We Hold.* Crestwood: St Vladimir's Seminary Press, 1980.

Michael Pomazansky. *Orthodox Dogmatic Theology: A Concise Exposition.* Platina: St Herman of Alaska Brotherhood, 1984.

Bishop Kallistos Ware. *The Orthodox Way.* Crestwood: St Vladimir's Seminary Press, 1979.

Further Resources are available from:

St Vladimir's Seminary Press (SVS Press)
575 Scarsdale Rd, Crestwood, NY 10707
(914) 961-8313

Light and Life Publishing Company
PO Box 26421, Minneapolis, MN 55426

Holy Cross Orthodox Press
 50 Goddard Ave, Brookline, MA 02146

St Tikhon's Seminary Press
 South Canaan, PA 18459

Antiochian Orthodox Christian Archdiocese Publications
 358 Mountain Rd, Englewood, NJ 07631

Orthodox Christian Publications Center (DRE)
 PO Box 588, Wayne, NJ

God has only revealed to us a tiny + only proportion of the Father, Son, + H.S. asking us to be faithful to that small bit which we know.